METHUEN'S MANUALS OF PSYCHOLOGY

(Founder Editor C. A. Mace 1946–68)
General editor H. J. Butcher

Attributes of Memory

Also by Peter Herriot
An Introduction to the Psychology of Language
Language and Teaching

ATTRIBUTES OF MEMORY

Peter Herriot

METHUEN & CO LTD
11 New Fetter Lane
London EC4P 4EE

First published 1974
by Methuen & Co Ltd
11 New Fetter Lane
London EC4P 4EE

© 1974 Peter Herriot
Typeset in Great Britain by
Preface Limited, Salisbury, Wilts.
and printed in Great Britain at the
University Printing House, Cambridge

ISBN hardbound 0 416 78870 X
ISBN paperback 0 416 70330 5

Contents

Preface

This book is intended for the later stages of undergraduate courses, but may also prove useful to postgraduate students. It is not an overall review, but rather a selective account of those areas of memory research which lend themselves to treatment in terms of coding by attributes. As a result, several areas receive little or no attention except where they fit into the overall argument. Little space is devoted to the field of attention, to recognition of words, to mathematical models of information processing, or to physiological aspects of memory. These omissions are not as important as they would otherwise be, since a forthcoming volume in this series will deal with them in depth. Developmental, pathological and motivational aspects are also largely omitted.

The absence of any form of diagram or figure throughout the text perhaps requires explanation. This book is intended to be read in conjunction with *Readings in Human Memory*, edited by J. M. Gardiner; experimental details have been omitted since this companion volume will provide the original published reports of many of the key experiments quoted. Moreover, the present writer feels that diagrams with little boxes and arrows are too likely to be misconstrued.

I would like to thank Barbara my wife for her encouragement and help; my friends and colleagues, Gus Craik, John Gardiner, Phil Johnson-Laird, Roy McConkey, and Steve Miller, for their helpful suggestions; and the chairman and staff of the Department of Special Education, Ontario Institute for Studies in Education, for study facilities and secretarial assistance. I would also like to apologize to Benton J. Underwood for borrowing the title of this book from his outstanding review article of 1969; no other title seemed appropriate.

CHAPTER 1

Introduction

1.1 Experimental psychology of memory

1.1.1 Experimental and 'natural' memory

The function of this first chapter is to orient the reader towards the concepts employed in the rest of the book. These will be defined more fully and evidenced in subsequent chapters. The first chapter aims at being a reasonably neutral introduction to conceptual terminology; the remainder presents a particular point of view.

Most experimental psychologists investigating memory have presented material of one sort or another to subjects and required them to recognize or recall it subsequently. The criterion of success is the recall or recognition of the correct material. Correctness is determined by the experimenter; in the recall task, the degree of correctness required is usually verbatim; that is, the subject has to recall the material in the form in which the experimenter presented it. More recently, some psychologists have required subjects to produce verbal or other behaviour which is derived from their general store of past experience rather than from a particular presentation by the experimenter. In this case there are seldom 'correct' responses. The objective is to obtain evidence concerning the structure of the subject's knowledge.

It is clear immediately that the way in which we use the words 'remember' and 'memory' in ordinary language is considerably wider than the experimental psychologist's usage. When we speak of someone remembering what another person said, we are usually talking about successful recall of the gist of the utterance, not a verbatim record. Moreover, we do not only speak of remembering something. We also remember how to do something, or when and where something happened. And we usually remember as a means to an end rather than as an end in itself. Why do the psychologist's and the layman's uses of the word differ so?

It may be asked, however, whether it is useful to have any labels at all for so-called areas of psychology. The existence of labels has led to the *decoupling* of one area from others (Reitman, 1970). Psychological processes have been termed learning processes, memory processes, or perceptual processes. Some of these distinctions may be valuable — for example, it may be useful to distinguish attention and perception from memory. However, there is always the danger that the areas are simply rationalizations of the use of different experimental techniques. The apparent conclusion to be drawn from such terminology is that, for example, memory processes and learning processes are different in kind from each other. Such a conclusion may not be justified.

Moreover, the decoupling of memory has resulted in an insularity in terms of both theory and practice. Until recently, for example, researchers into memory paid little attention to psycholinguistics. If a memory task requires subjects to employ linguistic skills, it is surprising if the experimenter does not take any account of what is known about them.

One alternative approach to the use of terms such as memory and learning is to adopt exclusively the analogy of the human being as the computer, the processor of information. Within the last fifteen years there has been a paradigm shift in psychology (Kuhn, 1962). The language or terminology of stimulus and response has been replaced by that of information processing. This has resulted in the strategy of using the input and the output of the human 'machine' as evidence from which to infer *how* the machine works. Less attention is paid to the question of *why* the machine works as it does, since this is regarded as logically subsequent. The computer analogy has been more successful in describing what is known than was the stimulus-response terminology. It has also given rise to a greater variety of research questions. However, mathematical information theory and measurement has not proved the unifying tool that it was at first expected to be. As a result, areas of research within the information processing area have become isolated. In particular, initial information processing and subsequent information processing have become very distinct from each other. Using older terminology, attention and perception have become distinct from memory and learning.

1.1.2 Pre-theoretical assumptions

There are, however, a great many more determinants of the contents of this book than the computer analogy. Experimental psychologists carry out their work with many, often unspoken, *pre-theoretical assumptions*. The very fact that they find it possible to use the analogy of a machine to describe at least part of the activity of human beings indicates certain assumptions. They are particularly concerned with making inferences about how the 'machine' works from what goes into it and what comes out of it. They will, therefore, pay particular attention to controlling the input by controlling the experimental situation, and to measuring the output, the behaviour of the subject. When they make inferences about how the 'machine' works, they will adopt a nomothetic rather than an idiographic approach; that is, they will be more concerned with making generalizations about how the human organism functions than with individual differences between people (e.g. Warr, 1973).

It must be stressed, however, that the use of the machine analogy does not imply any particular ethical or philosophical position. It is used purely as an heuristic device; that is, something which adequately describes the results of existing research and generates fruitful hypotheses. Experimental psychologists do not necessarily adopt a completely environmentalist view of human behaviour; they do not all assume that the machine produces a certain output of behaviour solely as a result of previous input. Nor is their purpose the sinister one of prediction and control of the subject's general behaviour. Their prediction is the statement of an expected outcome of a particular experiment, and their control is of the externals of the experimental situation.

The danger of the experimentalist's assumptions are all too clear. Because the input and the output are in the same form, he runs the risk of underestimating the extent to which the input has been transformed on its way through the machine. For example, given that he presented a subject with a list of words, and the subject subsequently recalled a large number of those words, it was not necessarily some physical copy that the subject stored and retrieved. There is an important distinction to be drawn, therefore, between the *nominal* and the *functional* stimulus. The former is the stimulus as the experimenter presents and defines it, the latter is the stimulus as coded by the subject. The subject acts upon or transforms the physical stimulus, and this is termed *coding* (see 1.3.1).

As a result of the underestimation of the difference between nominal and functional stimuli (i.e. of the extent of the subject's coding) a further unwarranted assumption has followed. It has been assumed that the limitations of the system are more important than its potential. Experimental psychologists have asked why we forget more often than they have asked how we remember. They have made tasks difficult by presenting un-related meaningless items at a fast rate, instead of giving the subject the opportunity to use the immense resources at his disposal in the leisured perusal of a meaningful whole. It is the main purpose of this book to redress the balance a little.

1.2 The human computer

1.2.1 Structure and process

Within the framework of the analogy of the human being as a processor of information, two basic emphases may be detected. The first concentrates upon the *structure* of the system, the second on the *processes* which must underly its successful function. In computer language, structure implies the hardware, the nature of the machine itself and the system it presupposes; process has affinities to the operations the computer performs, the sequence and identity of which is determined by the programme.

The structural emphasis places particular stress upon the nature of the system. It suggests that the nature of the system places constraints upon the rate of flow of information through it. The system, it is supposed, is of limited capacity. There are certain points in the flow diagram representing the system at which these constraints are strongest. Particular structures are hypothesized at these points in the flow diagram. For example, short-term and long-term stores are distinguished and placed in that order in the flow diagram. Moreover, the very use of a flow diagram may imply a *temporal sequence,* with information being passed through the system from one structure (e.g. short-term store) to another (e.g. long-term store). Thus the basic concepts of the structural emphasis are the structural constraints upon the transmission of information, which is conceived as a temporal sequence.

The second emphasis is on *process.* Within this emphasis we may distinguish two apparently contradictory components. The first is closely connected with the structural emphasis (Atkinson and Shiffrin, 1968). If the system is of limited capacity, particularly at certain points, then *control processes,* usually consciously applied, may be postulated which have the function of minimizing these limitations. So, for example, one of the functions of rehearsal of items in short-term memory is to retain information in temporary store until the system has free capacity to pass it along to a more permanent storage location. Similarly, a control process of selection is hypothesized. This has the function of filtering incoming information at an early stage in the system, so that irrelevant information is discarded as soon as possible. Clearly, both these control processes are made necessary by the supposed limitations on information flow imposed by the nature of the task. And both may be consciously applied in an effort to compensate for these limitations.

However, there is a second component in the process emphasis, an *elaborative* component which cannot be explained in the same way. For example, the *multiple* nature of the coding of items cannot be explained in terms of *reducing* load. It seems that subjects can and do encode material in many and various ways. Not only may they code it in terms of many aspects of the situation in which it was presented (e.g. 'What item was item x next to?', 'Was the voice that uttered the item male or female?', etc.). They may also code it in terms of a wide variety of other features or attributes. These may be the product of their previous experience organized into a cognitive and semantic system. So, for example, they may code the word 'dog' in terms of its attribute as a domestic animal. Such coding may not always be a consciously controlled process, but rather a swift and automatic one (Posner and Warren, 1972). Its function is to provide a set of attributes by which the item can be uniquely defined. Then, when recall or recognition is required, the item can be retrieved or reconstructed without being confused with any of the innumerable related items within the subject's experience. The emphasis is thus on *richness*, not on limitations; the richness of coding, and the richness of experience.

1.2.2 Short- and long-term stores

The emphasis on structural limitations and reductive coding will be considered first. Leaving aside the registration of input by the senses, two memory stores have been commonly distinguished, primary memory and secondary memory, or short- and long-term *stores* (Baddeley, 1972). These should be distinguished from short- and long-term memory *tasks*, which are defined by the length of time between presentation and recall. The distinction is between overt features of the task and postulated structures in the system. Primary memory and secondary memory have been distinguished in three ways. First, they are assumed to differ in capacity. Primary memory has a limited capacity, both in terms of amount of material and time of retention, while secondary memory has an essentially unlimited capacity. Second, they are assumed to differ in the type of coding which is applied to the information they contain. Primary memory has been assumed to favour a coding in terms of the physical or phonological characteristics of an item, whereas secondary memory favours one in terms of its meaning. Third, they are assumed to differ in the way items are lost from them, or forgotten. Primary memory loses items because they are overloading it, secondary because they are interfered with by other material.

The capacity limitations of primary memory are associated with the postulation of the control process of *rehearsal*. Rehearsal in its broader sense refers to the maintenance of material in a relatively uncoded form in order to minimize forgetting. It does not always result in overt vocalization; rather, it is a process that must be inferred from various other sorts of evidence.

1.2.3 Storage and retrieval

Another result of the structural approach, and in particular the notion of a long-term store, is the distinction between storage and retrieval. *Storage* is supposed to occur as the result of the selection and retention of presented material, while *retrieval* from store is considered a necessary condition for recall. Is this distinction justified?

One piece of evidence that it may be is the finding of Tulving and Pearlstone (1966). They discovered that there is a lot more memorised material *available* at the time of recall than is actually *accessible* (i.e. can actually be retrieved). By providing subjects with category cues at recall, e.g. 'animals', they increased considerably the number of items recalled successfully. This indicates that there is a discrepancy between what is stored and what is retrieved, and implies that the task of retrieval is worthy of investigation in its own right.

A second type of evidence often taken to indicate that it may be useful to distinguish between storage and retrieval is the superiority of *recognition* over recall performance. The recognition task requires the subject to identify items as having been presented earlier; the recall task requires him to reproduce such material. In the former, the subject is given some items and asked whether he saw them earlier. In the latter, he has to produce the items himself. Some psychologists (e.g. Kintsch, 1970a) have assumed that recognition performance is an index of the extent to which subjects have stored the material successfully. Therefore the inferiority of recall to recognition represents the extent to which storage and retrieval are more difficult than storage alone.

Finally, there are occasions when retrieval fails, and subjects retrieve attributes of to-be-recalled words only, or words related to them.

1.3 Coding

1.3.1 Reduction and elaboration coding

Now we consider the process, as opposed to the structural emphasis. In view of its centrality, the concept of coding processes requires further introduction and elaboration. The concept demands the distinction between the nominal and functional stimulus outlined earlier. It refers to the operations the subject performs upon the nominal stimulus in order to transform it into the functional one.

The nominal stimulus, the stimulus as presented, is first *registered* by the sensory systems. These retain a fairly liberal representation of the stimulus material for a short period of time, but during this period a great deal of material may be retained. The function of this sensory registration may be to retain material for a sufficient period for coding processes to act upon the physical stimulus and transform it.

The two basic aspects of coding processes are, first, the structural limitations upon the amount of information that can be processed at any one time; second, the variety of the coding processes available. These two aspects are reflected in the distinction between reduction and elaboration coding (Baddeley and Patterson, 1971). Reduction coding reduces the amount of material the subject has to process; elaboration coding adds to it. Both types of coding serve to assist recall performance: reduction coding by easing the information load on the system, elaboration coding by making material more distinctive from other material, and therefore more easily retrieved.

Reduction coding may take the form of *selecting* one from among many attributes of a presented stimulus item (see 3.4.1). If, for example, the nominal stimulus is a consonant-vowel-consonant (CVC) nonsense syllable, e.g. VUP, the functional stimulus as coded might be a phonemic representation of the second consonant, P.

A second form of reduction coding involves the *rewriting* of several items into a single coding (see 3.4.2). This coding therefore contains more information than each item individually, and may thus be used at recall to enable the items to be retrieved. The classic example in the experimental literature is given in Miller's well-known paper (1956). Material which consisted of long sequences of the binary digits 0 and 1 was recoded so that the digits 0 to 8 were used as codes for sequences of three binary digits. Thus for example, the sequence 000 was coded as 0, 001 as 1, 010 as 2, 100 as 3, etc. The recoding does not have to be in terms of the same symbol system as the items, however, or even the same modality. Both types of reduction coding have in common the function of easing the load on the processing system. They therefore tend to be used by the subject when the material is presented at a fast rate, and when the items to be recalled are not hard to discriminate from a large number of related items.

When they are hard to discriminate, *elaboration* coding will be useful. For elaboration coding enables the subject to retrieve the to-be-recalled item by providing enough features, or *attributes*, to distinguish it from other related but not-to-be-recalled items. For example, an item such as 'apple' might be encoded in terms of the fact that it occurred in the list after the word 'table', in terms of its sound attributes (e.g. it is disyllabic and starts with A), and in terms of its meaningful attributes (e.g. it is an edible fruit). This coding might successfully distinguish it from the other related items which the subject might wrongly retrieve, since, for the subject, that set of attributes might uniquely define 'apple'.

Items may not only be elaborated by being coded in terms of a number of attributes which the subject *extracts*. They may also be elaborated by features being *added* to them. For example, a verbally presented item may be coded into a complex visual image (see 3.3.1). Or a nonsense syllable (e.g. MOY) may be coded into a word (MOneY). However, this distinction between extracting several features from a nominal stimulus and adding features to that stimulus may be artificial; for in both cases the features are the products of the subject's coding process. The function of elaboration coding in general is to make items easier to distinguish from other items and therefore easier to retrieve.

The nature of the coding employed will probably depend upon the nature of the task. Where we have to recall material with which we are familiar, with codings which are highly related to many other codings, then elaboration coding is appropriate. It might be conjectured that most of our memorizing in daily life consists of producing material of this nature. It is also likely that prior elaboration coding may be a necessary condition for reductive coding to occur; the subject has first to code by several attributes in order to select a limited reductive coding consisting of a few of these attributes.

1.3.2 Multiple attributes and coding variability

One question that immediately arises concerns the *extent* of subjects' elaboration coding. Do they practise overkill, in the sense that they code items in many more ways than are needed to retrieve them successfully? Of course, parts of codings may be lost for various reasons in the course of time, so that overkill may be necessary if a sufficient coding is to be available when recall is required. However, the extent of coding is still a matter for debate. It will be shown later that some of the techniques used to investigate elaboration coding and the instructions they require may have led to an overestimate of the number of attributes into which a stimulus item is encoded (Underwood, 1972). It may be necessary once again to distinguish what a subject *can* do in an experimental task designed to give him every opportunity, and what he *does* do in the majority of tasks with which he is presented. One possibility might be that the subject selects certain sorts of coding to fit the demands of the presentation and recall situation (see 4.2.2). If he does not know when and in what circumstances he is going to have to recall, he may encode the material in many different ways to allow for different eventualities. Another possible explanation for multiple coding may be found in the distinction between *conscious and unconscious* (automatic) coding processes (Posner and Warren, 1972). It is possible that there is a level of automatic unconscious processing which subjects apply immediately an item is presented. Subsequently, conscious strategies may be employed, with the object of coding more effectively. The examples of stimulus selection and rewriting (see 1.3.1) are such conscious strategies.

The *encoding specificity* hypothesis (Thomson and Tulving, 1970) maintains that the coding used for retrieval of the item has to be the same as that used for its storage. Their experiments, which vary the cues for the to-be-recalled item at presentation and recall, show in general worse recall than when the same cues are provided at both phases of the experiment. However, as Bower (1972) points out, there may be many ways in which context is different at presentation and recall, apart from the cues actually provided by the experimenter. For example, the subject may be daydreaming about different things at the two phases of the experiment. Until we know exactly how subjects themselves code items (rather than how the experimenter can persuade them to), we cannot decide whether coding is specific or variable over time.

1.3.3 Episodic and semantic memory

Clearly, coding varies considerably in terms of nature and function; functional differences have already been discussed — whether the coding is reductive or elaborative. Another possibility is to distinguish episodic and semantic memory (Tulving, 1972).

Episodic memory refers to the use of coding attributes derived from the episode of presentation. For example, the item could be coded in terms of the fact that it was presented visually, not auditorily; that it occurred in List 1 rather than List 2; that it was nearer the beginning than the end of its list; that it was going to have to be recalled shortly, etc. In other words, episodic memory refers to personally experienced unique episodes.

Semantic memory, on the other hand, refers to the cognitive structure which is a result of *general* past experience and maturation. It deals with input not in terms of its perceptible features but in terms of its meaning detached from any specific experience. Thus the semantic memory system is supposed to be concerned with general items of knowledge, logical and linguistic rule-systems, and concepts and their relations. Therefore it provides attributes of, for example, a linguistic nature for the subject to use to code an item. He may, for example, code the visually presented shape of a bird with the name 'bird'; or he may code the auditorily presented word 'seagull' with, among other things, the attribute 'bird'; or he may code a sequence of numbers as even numbers, starting with four and increasing exponentially.

Thus, when material is presented and subsequent recall or recognition is demanded, coding attributes of both of these types can be applied. However, when a request is made for an item of knowledge or for a suitable word, the subject usually has to rely on his semantic memory alone. Thus, for example, if he is asked whether or not a canary is a bird, he has to use coding attributes of the word 'canary' which are semantic in origin (Collins and Quillian, 1969).

1.3.4 Levels of coding
Coding processes have been considered in terms of their reductive or elaborative function and in terms of their origin in the experimental episode or in semantic memory. Another important distinction is that between different levels of coding (Craik and Lockhart, 1972). It is supposed that some types of coding are 'deeper' than others. Some types of coding are useful when one sort of task is presented, other types when the task is different. So, for example, when the material is presented at a fast rate, when the items are not very meaningful and have few relations with each other, and when recall is to be demanded very shortly after presentation, then less deep coding may be applied. When, on the other hand, the material has a meaningful structure and is also closely related to other material which was not presented, and when recall is to be demanded after some interval, then a deeper level of coding may be preferable.

It seems possible that *episodic* memory might supply more of the attributes for coding when *less deep* levels, *semantic* memory when *deeper* levels, are required. Of course, an episodic memory task permits attributes derived from semantic memory to be used. As Tulving (1972) remarks, such attributes as order of presentation are very liable to loss through interference. Therefore material that is coded in terms of these attributes is liable to be forgotten very rapidly. On the other hand, such coding may take very little time both to apply and to decode. Often the phonological representation of the item (its name), together with a tag giving particulars of list membership and list position, may be adequate coding. Thus little time is taken up at storage and retrieval since little transformation of the material has to occur. Semantic coding, by way of contrast, involves the use of several attributes, both referential and affective. 'Black mamba' may be coded by its reptilian, poisonous, and fast-moving denotative attributes, and also by its evaluative and potency affective attributes. The construction of the uniquely defining set of attributes at storage, and the reconstruction of the item from those attributes at retrieval may take time. On the other hand, it might be less subject to interference and loss, and more efficient for retrieval purposes.

Thus it is possible that the notion of coding may lead to an emphasis on discovering how we remember in a wide variety of memory tasks, rather than why we forget under certain specific constraints.

1.4 Organization and control processes

1.4.1 Association

The terms 'association' and 'organization' are employed most frequently in cases where subjects are given lists of words which they have to recall in any order they wish. The experimenter may present the subjects with items, but the subject may code them in such a way that a number of items are grouped into a subjective unit. In other words, several nominal items are coded into one functional unit. The fact that these items have some attributes in common explains this form of coding. The terms 'association' and 'organization', used frequently in this area of research, both carry a heavy burden of meaning; they embody a large number of assumptions which are not always made explicit.

The concept of *association* owes its origin to learning experiments in which a stimulus was considered to become associated to its learned response. The adjacency of events in time is the key notion of associationism; in its completely empirical sense, it can be defined in terms of the probability of one event (a response) occurring, given another immediately prior event (a stimulus) (Postman, 1968). However, experiments which tried to devise situations in which connections between stimuli and responses had to be learned from scratch failed. This failure was due to the fact that previous experience always resulted in some form of coding of the stimulus, even though it might be a nonsense syllable. It gave rise to the concept of *implicit association*. It was supposed that other words related to the word or nonsense syllable presented in the experiment were elicited covertly in the experimental situation. That is, the subject responded implicitly to a stimulus word with other words derived from his existing language 'habits'. The implicit associates mediated between stimulus and response terms. These language 'habits' were described in terms of habit-family hierarchies, and, more recently, in terms of associative networks (Deese, 1965). The data upon which these theoretical constructs rest are largely derived from the technique of free association. Subjects are asked to say the first word that comes to mind on being presented with the stimulus. The word with which most subjects respond is considered to be a strong associate of the stimulus, while one with which relatively few subjects respond is a weak associate. Words are related to each other in associative networks, in terms of the number of associates they have in common. It is assumed that the *norms* derived from the explicit free association task represent the average *individual* subject's implicit associative network. For example, if white is the strongest associate to black, in the sense that more people respond with it than with any other word, then it is assumed that it is one of the most closely related words in the individual's network.

As Postman (1968) is careful to point out, such concepts as 'associative network' have a different status from concepts like 'implicit association'. The former is what the subject brings to the experimental situation. The latter is a dependent variable — the stimulus word may or may not elicit much of the network as implicit associations in a given experimental task.

The notion of implicit association suggests that the implicit 'responses' are verbal in nature, like the item presented. It therefore presupposes an identity of form in the nominal and the functional stimulus. Expressed in terms of coding, the stimulus word is being coded also in terms of other words; other words are acting as attributes.

However, there is another area of associative theory which does not make this presupposition. The whole basis of Osgood's semantic differential is *dimensional* (Pollio, 1968). That is, certain affective features of words are, it is suggested, the basis for implicit 'responses'. The position of a word along the three dimensions of evaluation, potency and activity defines that word in affective semantic space. Thus, in coding terms, the stimulus word is coded in terms of these dimensions.

Clearly, these constructs of associationist theory have potential value in describing how several items are coded into single subjective units. Firstly, the juxtaposition of items at presentation might result in their association, and the consequent use of one to cue the other in recall. Or, secondly, some of the items presented may be associated with each other in the subject's associative network; in this case, although they were not presented in juxtaposition, such items might be recalled together. Such association might be explained in terms of one item being directly elicited by another; or in terms of both items sharing common associates. Clearly, more than two items may be involved in the associative grouping, however. One item may directly elicit another, which in its turn directly elicits another. Or several items may share a common mediating associate or associates, so that all of these items are recalled together.

However, the major objection to associationist theory is its emphasis on the nominal stimulus. Except in the case of Osgood's semantic dimensions, the supposed codings (or mediating responses) tend to be of the same form as the overt stimulus. As will be seen in the next chapter, codings occur in a very wide variety of dimensions, some of them very far removed from the nature of the nominal stimulus. On the other hand, the notion of affective dimensions of meaning and the stress on the context of presentation are important contributions of associationist theory. The use of associationist terminology has decreased recently, perhaps because, as Postman (1972) remarks, 'organization theorists have asked many important and imaginative questions about the conditions of learning and recall that association theorists had not asked'.

1.4.2 Organization

The concept of *organization* derives from more specific origins than those of association. It has become popular since the experimental technique of *free recall* has become widely used. Free recall is free in the sense that it permits the subject to recall items in whatever order he wishes. Concentration may therefore be focused on the *order* of items in recall. Where any recognizable consistency occurs in this order, organization is assumed to have occurred. Clearly, this is an operational definition; it does not offer explanations for the consistency, just as the operational definition of association does not offer an explanation for the increase of probability of a response in the presence of a stimulus.

However, Tulving (1968) suggests possible bases for consistency in output order. He maintains that it occurs when the semantic or phonetic relations between items govern the order; or when the subject's acquaintance with the items either previous to the experiment or during it affects the sequential order of output. It may be that this definition of organization is limited by its origin in the free recall technique, and its consequent stress on order of recall. A more general definition would simply refer to the imposition of structure, without specifying its nature or the preferred evidence for it. Such a broad definition allows full weight to be given to results derived from other experimental techniques. In particular the *interference* paradigm (see 5.3.2 and 7.1.1) yields potential information about organization. If the learning of ten items negatively transfers to the learning of twenty, of which the ten are part, this implies organizational coding of items rather than the independent coding of each item. Such techniques provide evidence as to the nature of what is *learned*. The order of items in recall may be no more than a characteristic of *performance* (Postman, 1972). For it has been shown that subjects can order their recall according to instructions.

Thus the concept of organization is bound up with the distinction between nominal and functional. Although material is presented as items, subjects may code them in such a way as to make the functional unit larger than the item. In other words, the functional unit may be the coding of several items together — a coding, in fact, by means of attribute(s) common to them.

1.4.3 Subjective and imposed organization

The operational definition of organization has been stated above — consistency in order of items at output. This consistency has been observed in various ways. Firstly, the subject may order the items in terms of some feature which the *experimenter* has determined. The experimenter may, for example, select five animals, five fruits, five items of clothing, and five modes of transport. He may then present them to the subject in random order and observe the extent to which he recalls them in categorical order. In this case, the only organization with which the subject is credited is that which the experimenter has imposed. He has imposed it by selecting the items in terms of the categories, and by quantifying the order of recall in the same terms. He is thus looking for the reproduction by the subject of the organization he has himself imposed. To the extent that the subject imposes any *different* organization, he will be credited by the experimenter with *less*.

An alternative technique is to observe regularities in the subject's own ordering of randomly selected items over successive recall trials. The items are presented in one random order, then recalled. They are then presented in another random order, and recalled again; and so on. The subject may recall the same items in the same order on successive trials. This is taken as an index of the subjective organization. In both cases (with categorical and randomly selected material) *order* properties are assessed independently of *item* properties (amount recalled), thus rendering the relation between the two open to investigation.

The *interference* paradigm does not make use of measures of organization which depend on order of items in recall. By manipulating independent variables, one can regulate the nature and extent of the subject's organization of the interfering list. The differential effects on the recall of the interfered-with list can then be observed.

In general, the emphasis has been on experimenter-determined rather than subject-determined organization (Tulving, 1968).

1.4.4 Organization and amount recalled

Organization clearly has an important role to play in information processing. Consider, first, the structural emphasis within that analogy. It is supposed that the information processing system is by its very structure limited in capacity. Organization could therefore be seen as a means of reducing the load on the system. If several items can be coded by the attributes that they have in common, then this coding will take up less processing capacity. That is, the items can be stored and retrieved by means of their common coding, which is thus the basic unit that has to be retained. (On the other hand, it must also be explained how the *correct* items are retrieved, and not other related words — e.g. how the five presented animal words rather than other animal words are recalled.)

Mandler (1966) supposes that there are upper limits on the number of items which can be stored and retrieved by a single coding, and on the number of codings which can themselves be retained. This limit is expressed in the title of Miller's (1956) classic paper 'The magical number 7, plus or minus two' (see 1.3.1). However, it may be that this 'strong' hypothesis (Postman, 1972) is unjustified. For it has been shown that the number of functional units (groupings of items) which a person can remember and their size (the number of items per grouping) vary independently. This argues against a fixed and similar limit to memory for units and to memory for items per unit.

However, organization may not consist of distinct and separate groupings of items. Groupings may overlap. The same item may be coded into two or more functional units, depending upon which dimensions the units are based on. For example, the items 'cat' and 'dog' could both be coded semantically as domestic animals; 'dog' could be coded as occurring in the first third of the list, 'cat' in the middle; and both could be coded as monosyllabic, in contrast to other polysyllabic items. Thus in two out of three cases, the items were coded by the same value of the same feature, but in the third they were not. Moreover, the subjective units may differ in size; while there may be four categorical units of which the list is composed, there may be only three portions of the list — early, middle, and late — into which items are coded in terms of position.

Thus items may not be coded into clear-cut units; as a result, each item has more chance of being retrieved successfully when recall is demanded. For even though one of the functional units to which it belongs may not be retrieved at all, it may be recalled as part of another unit to which it also belongs.

Both the reductive and the elaborative features of organizational coding are thus aids to recall. Whichever of these two aspects is indexed by the measures of organization, correlations between degree of organization and amount recalled should result. However, most of the evidence of this positive relationship which has emerged has been taken to support the structural emphasis and its corollary, reductive coding. This is because of the nature of many free recall tasks, and the type of measure of organization employed. The tasks often require the subject to recall an equal number of items from various simple semantic categories, e.g. five animals, five fruits, five items of clothing, etc. And the measure is often an index of the extent to which subjects recall items from the same category adjacently. Thus what is measured is in fact simple reductive coding. Evidence for a positive relation between *complex* organization and amount recalled awaits either a satisfactory measure of complex organization or the discovery of those independent variables which reliably result in complex organization: their effect on recall could then be ascertained. Moreover, amount recalled (as expressed in terms of number of items) is itself a nominal rather than a functional measure. Therefore correlations between order and item properties confound functional and nominal indices.

1.4.5 Control processes, retrieval plans and rules

In memory experiments, subjects differ from each other in their response to a particular task; each subject makes different responses to different tasks; he may even make different responses over time to the same task. He may, for example, stop rehearsing items in the order in which they are being presented, and try to use a mnemonic system instead; or he may stop coding in terms of semantic coding and employ rhyming features instead; or he may stop trying to visualize a page of lecture notes and start trying to locate the material required in the context of the lecture in which it was presented. In other words, *selection* from among alternative control processes is implied.

Such selection is presumably derived from feedback and is aimed at meeting a subjectively imposed criterion. If one agrees that alternative strategies are open to subjects, then the choice of only one dimension for measurement by the experimenter (e.g. semantic categories) has obvious limitations. For it is only sensitive to the use of one particular strategy. This selection appears to make it necessary to postulate different levels of control process, a high-level process involving the selection of lower-level processes (Reitman, 1970).

A second concept currently receiving much attention is that of *retrieval plans*. Coding of a set of items may be reductive or elaborative. Even when it is reductive, one still has to explain how the subject has available at recall the coding by which to retrieve the items. How, in other words, does he retain coded information? Even when the interval between presentation and recall is short, there is a limit to the number of codings he can rehearse or otherwise retain. It has therefore been supposed that he employs codings of codings to help him retrieve more immediate codings and then items. A retrieval plan is conceived of, therefore, as a way of decoding through different stages of coding until the subject can reconstruct the whole of the sequence of items presented (Wood, 1972). That subjects *can* use such retrieval schemes is shown by experiments in which superordinate, subordinate, and sub-subordinate words are presented in hierarchical form and recalled better as a result. Whether they *do* use such clear-cut methods remains to be seen, particularly if items are coded into more than one subjective unit. Moreover, there is a danger of an infinite regression: how do subjects retain codings of codings of codings of. . .?

The pre-existing systems of knowledge which subjects bring to the experimental situation are very hard to characterize because of their varied nature. It is perhaps possible to distinguish the *content* of particular systems from the *rules* for their use. Thus, for example, the content of the linguistic system may consist of elements, the combination of which is subject to rules. One can only order words grammatically in certain ways; one can only use a word in conjunction with some, but not all, other words. The important feature of rules is their *productivity*. That is, they can be used to generate sequences of elements which have never been generated before. The sentence I am now writing may be a completely novel event. This feature of rules is not confined to linguistic rules. There are rules of inference, which, however, may not follow strictly logical patterns. We may also have many more specific rule systems, such as, for example, the ordering of items along a continuum of magnitude, or the ordering of words in alphabetic sequence. As Tulving (1972) suggests, 'a person may have never learned that March follows June in the alphabetical listing of months, and yet be able to retrieve this bit of knowledge upon an appropriate query'.

However, the danger of adding concept to concept in an effort to explain complex phenomena must now be evident. The notions of control processes, strategies and rules, for example, are useful for heuristic purposes. That is, they lead to the asking of useful questions. But the real search is for the processes that regulate behaviour. It is always tempting to infer that a conceptual distinction or an experimental method signifies the discovery of a process. Such inferences are usually false. The only way in which psychological processes are experimentally evidenced is by prediction and control. We must be able to explain findings parsimoniously in terms of a particular construct (e.g. strategies), and we must find it difficult or impossible to find an equally parsimonious alternative.

The position adopted in this book is to emphasize the notion of coding by attributes. It will be argued that only a strong emphasis on the discrepancy between the nominal and the functional stimulus does justice to the evidence. Of particular weight is the evidence concerning how we organize lists of items into quite different units. The necessary result is a concentration on processes and their products. The processes involve both the transformation of the nominal stimulus into an abstract coded form, and also subsequent operations upon the abstract attributes thus produced. The title of this book thus reflects an emphasis on the products of the coding process. This approach is considered preferable to an emphasis on structural features exemplified in the distinction between short- and long-term stores. For, as will be shown in Chapter 7, there are alternative explanations of the evidence cited in favour of this distinction.

5 Summary

The first chapter has served, however, as an introduction to some of the conceptual distinctions employed in memory research. It must be admitted that it is a partial introduction; partial in the sense that it is not impartial, and also in the sense that several concepts are not mentioned. Both types of partiality are the result of the writer's theoretical bias. The richness of the coding process has probably been overemphasized at the expense of the structural limitations; the difference between nominal and functional characteristics may have been exaggerated; more stress has been laid on organizational coding than on coding of individual items; and the loss of items (forgetting) has been almost completely ignored, as has the traditional theoretical account of forgetting in terms of interference.

It was suggested that the term 'memory' was justifiably used to describe an area of psychological research. This was because its richness of meaning has recently forced psychologists to ask important questions. It was seen that the analogy of the computer, the human being as a processor of information, dominated research as the current paradigm. The assumptions underlying the use of this analogy were explored, with particular reference to the effects they have had on the questions asked by memory researchers and the methods they have employed. Much research has been derived from particular research techniques rather than from general theoretical standpoints. Further, the distinction between the nominal and the functional stimulus has not always been recognized.

The two basic emphases of the computer analogy were contrasted, and described in terms of structure and process. The structural emphasis was seen to draw attention to the limitations of the human being as a processor of information. The process emphasis stresses the variety of codings and strategies which subjects use. The former, the structural, emphasis has given rise to the distinction between primary and secondary memory (short- and long-term stores), with primary memory conceived of as a store with limited capacity and duration. It has also led to the conception of reductive coding, whereby the items as presented are reduced into a form requiring less 'space' in the system. The latter emphasis, the process emphasis, has led to a particular concentration upon retrieval. It has been proposed that only when an item has been multiply coded can it be distinguished from other related items in the semantic system and thus successfully retrieved. Elaborative coding has been assumed to serve this purpose. However, it was seen that major problems awaited solution: for example, what is the extent and variability of subjects' codings; and whether subjects have to retrieve items by exactly the same codings as they use to store them.

Two related distinctions were noted; that between episodic memory (of events in one's experience) and semantic memory (one's body of linguistic knowledge); and that between deep and less deep levels of coding. It was proposed that different levels of coding were appropriate for different tasks, and that semantic memory might provide more of the attributes for deep, the episode of presentation for less deep levels of coding.

Organizational coding, by which codings are applied in such a way as to relate items to each other, was discussed at length. The concepts of association theory were seen to be applicable to many of these cases, but associationist terminology was rejected in favour of organization as a unifying concept. This was because associationism appeared to minimize unduly the difference between nominal and functional characteristics; and because the organization terminology appeared to lead to more fruitful experimental hypotheses. The organization terminology had resulted firstly in a stress on the order of items in free recall; and secondly in the recognition that the organization which the experimenter expected to find and tried to measure might differ considerably from the organization which the subject himself applied. It was suggested that degree of organization might be positively related to amount recalled for two reasons. It might reduce the load on the system, since it was reductive in nature; or it might aid retrieval because of the membership of the item in several different subjective organizational units.

Finally, it was stressed that various selection and control processes had to be postulated to account for the variety of strategies employed by subjects. It was also pointed out that the nature of semantic memory has to be specified; and that one possible theoretical construct was that of generative rules.

The remaining chapters have the following rationale. Chapters 2 and 3 describe the various forms of coding which have been evidenced, with Chapter 2 dealing with less deep, Chapter 3 with deeper forms. Chapter 4 discusses some of the problems that arise as a result of the use of the concept of coding and the research it has generated. Chapter 5 refers specifically to the coding of lists of items. Chapter 6 makes an effort to characterize the systems of knowledge which must be supposed to underly the subject's ability to use codings. Chapter 7 places the coding terminology in the context of the development of theories about memory, and argues in favour of rejecting the distinction between primary and secondary memory. The concept of different levels of coding is preferred as an orienting framework for future research.

CHAPTER 2

Surface forms of coding

The concept of coding is central to the argument of this book. Coding implies an active experimental subject, who transforms the nominal into the functional stimulus. Chapters 2 and 3 provide an account in some detail of the evidence which supports the hypothesis that such coding occurs. Different forms or types of coding are distinguished; they are arranged in the chapters in a sequence from apparently lesser to apparently greater complexity of coding operations. This arrangement is not based on substantial evidence in detail, although, as will be seen in Chapter 4, coding on the basis of physical features of the stimulus may be less effective than coding on the basis of meaning. Little theoretical argument is included in Chapters 2 and 3; their function is to review evidence. Reference back to these chapters will occur frequently in later chapters, where research described in them will be cited in support of the coding approach. The order of Chapters 2 and 3 carries no implications about surface forms of coding occurring before deeper forms of coding, or being in any sense more basic or 'scientific'.

2.1 Sensory registration

2.1.1 The partial report technique
It was suggested in the previous chapter that it might not be appropriate to consider human information processing in terms

of a flow diagram. One of the reasons for this suggestion was that a flow diagram implies a *sequence* of events in time, with one event being the necessary condition for the next. It will become evident from Chapter 4 that there is a lot of evidence against such a predetermined sequence. However, there is one event which *is* a necessary precondition for any further information processing to occur. This is the *registration* by the senses of the presented material.

Thus the first section of a chapter on coding processes concerns a fairly literal representation of the material presented. Sensory registration does not involve any basic transformation of the material. Some of the physical features are registered, and their representation is not changed from e.g. a visual to an auditory form. Thus the subject has available raw material on which to work. He may select some for further processing and discard the rest. The very possibility of selection implies some form of coding or identification in order for the criterion of selection or rejection to be applied to the items presented. Further coding appropriate to the memory task may then follow this selection. However, the function of the initial registration seems to be to make available to the subject as much of the presented material as possible for a limited period of time.

Any experimental technique which aims at revealing the existence of sensory registration must obtain a response from the subject immediately after presentation of the material. Previous experiments in which an array of items had been presented visually required subjects to report all the items they had seen after they were removed. Such a report took some time, and therefore one might expect some items to be lost during the period in which recall was taking place. The importance of the *'partial report'* technique devised by Sperling (1960) is that it overcomes this difficulty.

Sperling presented tachistoscopically for up to half a second an array consisting of three rows of letters. Immediately after the display had been removed, the subject was given a high-, moderate- or low-pitched tone as a signal. The function of the tone was to indicate which of the three rows the subject was to report. Clearly, the subject did not know until after the display had disappeared which row he would have to recall. Therefore one might expect his performance on the required row to be typical of the performance he would have managed on the two non-required rows. Thus the degree of his registration of the display as a whole may be estimated from his performance on a single row.

The results indicated nearly 100 per cent perfect recall of individual rows, whereas when recall of all the items is required, performance seldom reaches more than 50 per cent correct. The inference clearly is that all the items were registered, but that the total number of items registered was greater than could be retained during the time taken to recall.

Many questions immediately arise. How can one tell that it is in fact only the physical features of the display which are registered? How long does the registered material remain for use? What variables determine the length of time it remains? What use does the subject make of it while it is available to him?

Thorough exploitation of the partial report technique has provided tentative answers to some of these questions (Coltheart, 1972). For example, the length of time between the removal of the display and the signal has been varied. When the signal occurs half a second or more after removal, there is no advantage of the partial report over the full report procedure. It may be inferred that the representation is lost extremely rapidly in these conditions.

The nature of the part of the display which the subject has to report was varied also. Clearly, if a feature of the display is the basis for distinguishing the to-be-reported items from others, that feature must have been registered. The initial experimental technique showed that position (rows) was registered. It has subsequently been shown that the colour of the items, their shape and their size are also registered: subjects successfully reported a subsection of the display distinguished from other subsections by each of these features.

The specifically visual nature of this form of registration is indicated by the additional use of a flash of light. If this or a random pattern is presented immediately after the display, the subject cannot subsequently report the items. Moreover, if the visual field at which the subject looks in the interval between removal of display and signal to report is dark rather than light, then gaps of up to five seconds can occur without the loss of the representation (it will be recalled that the representation is lost within half a second when the visual field is light). Increasing the luminance of the display or the length of presentation also results in longer retention. Clearly, then, registration does not necessarily have a set and very short existence. But its visual nature is placed beyond doubt; so much so that Neisser (1967) termed this type of registration 'iconic memory', to contrast it with the comparable auditory registration ('echoic memory').

Further uses of these experimental techniques will be discussed later. This is because they shed light on coding rather than on sensory registration *per se*. Clearly, in the partial report procedure the registered items have to be coded (e.g. given a name) in order to be reported. Therefore the variables which have been manipulated in an effort to reveal registration may also be useful in shedding light on coding. For they may have effects upon coded 'read-out' from registration. This is particularly true of the technique of 'backward masking', that is, the presentation of a second stimulus other than a signal after the display has been removed.

2.1.2 The suffix technique

The same partial report technique cannot be employed so effectively with auditorily presented material, since large numbers of items cannot be presented simultaneously in that modality. Nevertheless, successful efforts have been made to present a limited number of items from three different spatial sources, then to demand a partial report from one of them (Darwin, Turvey and Crowder, 1972). An ingenious alternative to the partial report technique has been used by Crowder and Morton (1969); its exploitation has been similarly thorough, and is reported by Morton (1970).

Crowder and Morton postulate a 'precategorical acoustic store'; precategorical is taken to refer to the absence of complex coding operations. Like iconic memory in the visual modality, this store is taken to register items by their sensory properties without further coding, in this case, the acoustic rather than the visual properties are registered. The precategorical acoustic store would thus act as follows. Suppose a subject is presented auditorily with a few items sequentially ordered, his task being to recall them immediately afterwards in the correct order. The store would retain the sound of the experimenter's or the subject's own voice. This retention period would be long enough to preserve a record of the sound while the earlier items were being recalled. Then this record would permit the later items to be coded verbally and recalled in their turn. The function of the precategorical acoustic store would thus be similar to that of the iconic memory — retaining a physical representation of items for long enough to permit their coding.

Crowder and Morton employed the stimulus suffix and response prefix techniques. A stimulus suffix is an additional 'item' in the presented sequence of digits. It is, however, totally predictable to the subject (e.g. it would consist regularly of the word 'zero'), and its recall is not required. It thus resembles the visual mask employed by Sperling; like his flash of light or visual noise, it serves to intervene between presentation and recall in such a way as to erase the sensory registration of the items.

The first point to establish is that the suffix is acting upon the sensory registration of the presented material rather than interfering with the subject's recall. This is where the response prefix comes in. The response prefix is the requirement of the utterance of a completely familiar response item, e.g. 'zero', before the subject starts recalling the items. It results in worse performance *throughout* the sequence. This effect is attributable to interference with the making of the response. The stimulus suffix effect results in worse performance *at the end* of the list only. It is therefore different in kind from the response prefix effect, and requires a different explanation. Clearly, it points to a temporary acoustic registration, since only the most recently heard words are erased.

Manipulation of the nature of the suffix should lead to further information about the nature of acoustic registration. The presentation of the suffix in a different modality to the list results in the absence of the effect, indicating that the effect is modality specific (Morton and Holloway, 1970). Certain other results emphasize the specifically physical, acoustic properties of precategorical acoustic store. If, for example, the stimulus list is presented auditorily by a male speaker, but the suffix by a female speaker, the suffix effect is decreased. In other words, the extent of the erasure from acoustic registration is decreased. Similarly, items were presented visually, and the subject was required to read them aloud. Then, before recall, either the experimenter or the subject had to utter the word 'zero'. The last items were recalled worse only when the subject uttered the word 'zero'. In other words, his own utterance of 'zero' interfered more with the acoustic representation of his reading aloud, presumably because it was the same voice. In another experiment stressing the physical channel of the registration, the sequence of digits was presented to one ear and the suffix to the other. This resulted in better performance on the last items than when both digits and suffix were presented to the same ear. This indicates that one of the features registered acoustically is the particular input 'channel' by which the material is presented. Thus it may be concluded that physical features of the presentation such as pitch are registered, and that registration is and the channel through which presentation occurs may be registered.

As in the case of iconic memory, the acoustic registration appears to fade rapidly. When the suffix is delayed, it has no effect on the last three items. The suffix is normally presented at the same rate as the digits. So, for example, if the digits are presented at the rate of two per second, the suffix occurs half a second after the last digit. If it does not occur until two seconds after the last digit, it has no effect upon the recall of the last three digits.

There is one basic difference between iconic memory and the precategorical acoustic store, however. It seems probable that the type of acoustic registration evidenced by the suffix effect is specific to speech material. For when the suffix consists of a burst of loud white noise, it has no effect on recall of the last three items. This is in marked contrast to the erasing effect of a flash of white light upon the iconic store. But although the suffix effect may be specific to speech material, the more meaningful aspects of speech are not involved. Variations in the meaning, frequency of occurrence, or emotionality of the suffix employed have no effect on the extent of the suffix effect (Morton, Crowder and Prussin, 1971).

On the other hand, research using other forms of material presented auditorily (Massaro, 1970a) does show that a tone can be an effective mask. When, for example, the subject's task is to identify a very brief tone as either high or low in pitch, an immediately subsequent tone results in very poor performance; best performance is obtained when the masking tone is delayed for a quarter of a second. It is possible, then, that when auditory masking is involved, like is only masked by like, speech by speech, tone by tone. Discriminability may be involved.

2.1.3 Sensory registration and coding

It was suggested that the function of sensory registration was to retain presented material for long enough for it to be coded. The wide variety of features which are registered ensures that there is plenty of 'raw material' for coding processes to act on. The registration itself does not appear to involve meaningful coding. One piece of evidence suggesting that this is so involves the simultaneous use of both letters and digits in the visual array. When digits as opposed to letters were required as a partial report, performance was not superior to that on report of the whole array. This implies that the processing of anything other than the physical attributes does not occur as part of sensory registration.

However, it is also clear that such coding does occur, and that it occurs as soon as sensory registration has taken place. In other words, subjects start coding before the signal as to which subset of items they should report. Then they switch to the required subset, and start processing it in order to be able to report it. This is evident from the fact that subjects do report four or five items in the Sperling task even when the signal is delayed until after the period for which the registration lasts in this experimental situation. Further supporting evidence that subjects code items before the signal is that the signalled material is better reported when the non-signalled material is easily codable.

It also appears at first sight that items are coded extremely rapidly. For three items can be reported after an exposure of only fifty milliseconds, followed by a visual noise mask. Since the mask would remove the registered material, it follows that the coding must have occurred within the fifty milliseconds. However, it might be argued that the mask merely degrades the stimulus representation, the degrading effect becoming progressively weaker with mask delay. If this were the case the stimulus—mask interval would not correspond to the time available for coding.

This evidence may imply that it is not possible to equate the *coding* of the item with *naming* it subvocally, since naming would take far longer (perhaps about 100 milliseconds per monosyllabic item). A closer look at the effect of exposure duration upon amount recalled shows that for the first 50 milliseconds, amount recalled increases from zero to three items. In the next 100 milliseconds, on the other hand, average amount recalled increases by less than one item. This suggests the possibility that different forms of coding are occurring; the first is extremely rapid but of limited capacity, the second far slower.

The selective effect of backward masking supports the same inference. If a row of eight letters is followed by a visual noise mask, the effect of the mask is only upon the middle letters of the row. This suggests that the first and last items are already coded by the time the mask occurs; the coding of the remainder is dependent upon registration, and is therefore rendered impossible by the mask. The longer the exposure duration, the greater the number of items coded before the mask, and hence unaffected by it. However, this is only true up to 100 milliseconds, after which this increase in number of items coded is very small. Once again a very rapid form of coding, but one of only limited capacity, is implied.

It will be suggested in the subsequent sections that this rapid form of coding is visual in nature, whereas the slower form of coding is verbal naming. But it does not follow that all visual coding is short lived.

2.2. Visual matching and coding

2.2.1 Levels of abstraction

This section (2.2) describes the work of Posner, whose review article (1969) may be consulted for further details. Consider the visual presentation of the letter A to a subject. He may process that visual input in terms of its physical configuration. He may code it visually as a member of a class of visual forms of which members are Я A A. He may code it verbally by its name, 'a'. Or he may code it conceptually as a vowel rather than a consonant, or a letter rather than a digit. Posner describes these forms of coding as different levels of abstraction. By abstraction he refers both to the fact that subjects select features or attributes of the stimulus by which to code it; and also to the fact that the deeper the level of abstraction, the greater the number of specific examples the coding subsumes. Thus, for example, in order to code A visually, the subject has to pick out those features of A by which it is encoded as a capital A, as are all the other forms of capital A. Moreover, when the subject encodes a presented A as a verbal 'a', that coding subsumes all examples of the letter; it could, for example, be used to generate any number of different capital or lower case A's or a's.

It should be stressed that it is not assumed that these different levels of coding are mutually exclusive, either in the sense that one level cannot occur if another has been applied; or in the more restricted sense that a coding which succeeds another in order of time obliterates that prior coding. Rather, it will be shown that different levels of coding can be applied in parallel. The relations of these levels of coding have been elucidated in a brilliant series of experiments by Posner and his colleagues in which the matching technique has been exploited to the full.

This technique requires the subject to recognize identity between two items. He has to indicate whether the items are the same or different by pressing one of two keys. The dependent variable is the reaction time. The advantage of the technique is that the response is a simple binary choice regardless of the degree of complexity of the input. Thus the letters A and A will be rated as different when the task is to match according to physical identity; and the letters A and e will be rated as the same when the task is to match according to whether they are both vowels or not. The length of time required to make the binary decision will be an index of the time taken to code the stimuli at the level of coding selected by the experimenter.

2.2.2 Physical identity matching
The task of physical identity matching is a good example of the technique at work; it is also worthy of consideration in its own right. One use of the technique is to compare the time required for a physical identity match with the time required for a 'name' match (i.e. 'Do the two visually presented letters have the same name or not'). Subjects took 70 to 100 milliseconds less to respond when the items AA were presented for the former task than they did to respond when they were for the latter. Clearly, the inference is that subjects can match stimuli on the basis of physical identity faster than they can on the basis of name.

Further evidence suggests that the physical match is not influenced by the name. For when the stimuli under physical match instructions are Aa, it takes no longer to rate them different than it does to rate Ab different. Indeed, *no* form of prior familiarity appears to affect physical identity matching, since subjects can match unfamiliar nonsense figures as rapidly as letters. One final variation of the matching task indicates the importance of the physical identification of the stimuli.

Letters — for example, Aa and Cc — were presented under name match instructions. The former (Aa) took longer than the latter (Cc). And Cc took longer than CC or cc. Clearly, A and a are less physically similar than C and c; but even Cc requires compensation for size variation. Thus the ease of physical identification of stimuli affects the speed with which names are applied. Therefore the physical identity matching task has shown more than the existence of sensory registration. It has demonstrated relations between sensory features and ease of coding.

2.2.3 Specific visual coding

The variations of the matching technique described up till now have involved the presentation of the two items simultaneously in close proximity. Other variations present the items some distance apart, or with a time interval of up to two seconds separating presentation of each item. The task was to make a name match, and the items were presented for long enough (half a second) for subjects to produce a name code. The items were either physically identical (AA), had the same name (Aa), or were different (AB,Ab). Results showed that AA was matched about ninety milliseconds faster than Aa when there was no interval between items. There was a decrease in this difference as the interval increased, until with a two-second interval there was no difference at all. This implies that a visual coding as well as a name was extracted at the presentation of the first item, but that this coding no longer aided the match after two seconds. One possible inference is that the visual coding is effectively lost completely, or becomes inaccessible or 'noisy'.

Why should it be assumed that this visual coding is any different from the sensory registration evidenced by Sperling? If it is no different, the term 'coding' should not be used of it. The brief answer is that it is not affected by the same physical independent variables as is iconic memory. A patterned visual noise mask presented between the two stimuli has no effect on matching time, nor do variations in the luminance of presentation and its duration. Moreover, in a variation of the basic technique, four items were presented in a row. The subject's task was to say whether a 'probe' letter which appeared subsequently in one of the four positions had the same or a different name as the letter which had been in that position. The superiority of the physically identical items was only evidenced for the first two items in the row, suggesting that the visual code was only generated for two of the four items. This limitation is in marked contrast to the iconic memory, which has considerable capacity (e.g. sixteen out of eighteen items).

Other evidence indicates that a visual coding can be maintained for quite long periods. Kroll, Parks, Parkinson, Bieber and Johnson (1970) presented subjects with a letter of the alphabet either visually or auditorily. Then they required them to repeat a series of digits one by one after the experimenter. Finally they required recall of the letter. They found that memory for the visually presented letter was usually correct after ten or twenty seconds, and was significantly superior to recall of the auditorily presented letter. Recognition memory tasks show that such specific visual codings can last for periods of several minutes (Hintzman and Summers, 1973). Thus *maintenance* of the visual coding can span quite a lengthy period; but actual *application* of the visual coding appears to take place only when the material is being presented. Shaffer and Shiffrin (1972) gave subjects the task of recognizing pictures. Subjects were more confident in their recognition the longer each picture had been exposed to them; but varying the interval between each picture presentation had no effect.

2.2.4 Abstract visual coding

However, it must be noted that reaction time for Posner's matching task increased with inter-stimulus interval up to two seconds. The specific visual coding, in other words, is hard to maintain over any length of time. One possible explanation runs as follows. The visual coding is very rapidly assimilated into the abstract schema of the letter in question. The particular visual coding of A becomes quickly assimilated into a general stored abstraction of the letter, based upon previous experiences of A, A̅, ꓮ, *A*, and maybe of *a*, a, etc. In this case, therefore, a precise physical match is no longer possible, since the first letter has been transformed before the second letter is presented. The subject therefore has to match an abstraction with a more specific coding of the second letter; or alternatively, he has to wait until the abstract schema of the second letter is produced. It may well be more profitable to match on a verbal, name coding basis than on a visual coding basis if this is the case.

Evidence that it may be is provided by yet another variation of the basic technique: presentation of the first letter may be auditory or visual, while presentation of the second is always visual. It was reasoned that if there was such a general abstract schema of a letter, it should be activated by an auditory presentation of that letter. Therefore matching performance with auditory presentation of the first letter should be no worse than performance with its visual presentation. In fact, auditory presentation was not significantly worse than visual.

That the auditory presentation gives rise to an abstract visual code is also suggested by further manipulations within the above procedure. It makes no difference if the second (visual) letter is capital or lower case, even when subjects are told to consider the first (auditory) letter as a capital. The inference must be that the abstract code is general enough to include instances of both capitals and lower-case letters.

However, the processes of generating the abstract code from auditory and visual presentation may differ. Specifically, the coding of a visual presentation may involve a gradual loss of visual detail, while that of an auditory presentation will be directly into the abstract schema. This leads to the prediction, which is confirmed by the evidence, that the visual presentation will lead to better physical identity matching when the inter-stimulus interval is zero; all the detail is still available. However, this superiority is not evidenced when the inter-stimulus interval is lengthened to one second. By this time, the visual stimulus will have become abstracted into the same general schema that the auditory stimulus evokes. One general objection, however, to the notion of an abstract visual schema is that much of the above evidence can equally well support the inference of a name code.

2.2.5 The independence of visual and name codes

The inference that the visual and name codes for letters were independent would follow from the finding that certain independent variables affected one but not the other. These findings were obtained in the following way. A list of eight items was presented auditorily, which subjects had to recall after an intervening matching task. The usual matching task with physically identical items or items with the same name was presented, inter-stimulus interval being zero or two seconds. Thus subjects had a memory load of name-coded items to maintain while they were engaged in the matching task. Results showed that these subjects increased in their reaction times on the name match as inter-stimulus interval increased. A control group without the memory load showed no such increase. Moreover, the presence or absence of the name-coded memory load had no effect on physical identity matching (the index of *visual* coding).

The visual coding was affected by a different sort of experimental manipulation. An array was presented, followed by a probe in one of the positions of the array. The surrounding positions to the probed position were filled either with letters similar to the target letter in physical shape, or in sound, or in neither. The presence of the physically similar context led to increased reaction times for the physical identity match over the other sorts of context. The same was not true for the name match.

These results indicate that verbal confusion acts on the name code only, visual confusion on the visual code only. The stored codes are thus separate.

In summary, the exploitation of the matching technique by Posner has made it possible to distinguish visual and verbal coding of visually presented material. He has shown that these codes are independent of each other. Moreover, they may occur simultaneously (but see Sternberg, 1966). The presence of one form of coding does not necessarily obliterate the other, since even after an item has been named, subjects may still retain its visual coding. The nature of visual coding may become progressively more abstract over time, as the physical representation loses its specificity and acquires the characteristics of the general visual schema of the letter. The results do not indicate that visually presented material of a verbal nature *must* be coded verbally. Nor do they suggest that visual codes are only employed in situations where the retention required is of limited duration.

2.3 Acoustic and articulatory coding

2.3.1 Acoustic confusions
Posner employed visually presented letters in an effort to distinguish a visual from a verbal coding. There is a large body of work (reviewed by Sperling and Speelman, 1970) which throws more light on the sound characteristics of the verbal coding of letters, and also on the coding of words by their sound characteristics.

This work derives from an initial series of experiments by Conrad (1964). He presented visually series of six letters, and the subjects' task was to recall them by writing them down in the order in which they had been presented (serial recall). Thus at no point were the latter names uttered aloud. The basic data are the confusions which subjects make in recall, substituting an incorrect letter for the correct one in a given position in the sequence. These confusions can be tabulated in a matrix, indicating the relative frequency with which incorrect letters have been recalled in the position of a given letter. It was shown that letters which were similar to the correct letter in sound (e.g. c for p) occurred as confusions significantly more often than letters which were similar in shape (e.g. E for F). This implies that subjects coded the visually presented letters verbally by means of letter names; and that it is the sound characteristics of the letter names that are the features of this coding.

However, it must be stressed that the effect obtained is upon *order* information. That is, it is the order of recall rather than the recall of individual items that is disrupted by acoustic confusions. Just as many acoustically similar items are recalled as acoustically dissimilar ones. The first task of subsequent work was therefore to show that the effect was not due to a failure in rote sequencing. For a traditional associationist explanation would maintain (Wickelgren, 1965) that the sequence was rote-learned, with each item acting as a cue to the next. The errors in serial recall would then be the result of the acoustically similar items acting as ambiguous cues; the subject is not sure which item should follow an item because he is not sure of the latter's identity. However, Baddeley (1968) showed that this is not the correct explanation. For one would hypothesize on Wickelgren's associative hypothesis that errors would *follow* a letter which was acoustically similar to another letter in the list. Baddeley found that this was not the case in lists where there were some acoustically similar letters and others which were different to each other. On the contrary, it was the acoustically similar letters *themselves* that became confused in recall. This result supports the view that the subject's difficulty is in deciding what item to select, rather than where he is in the sequence. In other words, the codings of the similar items are themselves similar, and therefore it is harder to decide which is the right item to retrieve. Baddeley's experiment also showed that the same effects were obtained when the presentation was auditory and the material consisted of words rather than letters.

Further characteristics of the codings of the letters were revealed by Wickelgren (1966). He showed that the codings of letter names were not all-or-none, unitary phenomena. Rather, they consisted of bundles of distinctive features. The letter names P and B, for example, differ by only one distinctive feature: B is voiced and P is voiceless. Distinctive features have been specified by linguists (Jakobson and Halle, 1956). They are binary in nature, few in number, and, in combination, can probably generate all the known speech sounds in any language. They refer to characteristics of sounds, for example whether they are sibilant, plosive, etc.; they also refer to the place in the articulatory apparatus which is most prominent in their production, for example the lips, the teeth, or the palate. Wickelgren showed that even within a series of letter names that sounded similar (e.g. B, C, P, D, T, V, G), acoustic confusions were more likely to occur between letters that differed by only one distinctive feature than between those that differed by two; and so on. The inference is that the coding of a letter name or word by its sound is in terms of a bundle of distinctive features.

2.3.2 Articulatory versus acoustic coding

However, it is not clear whether the coding is acoustic or articulatory in nature (Wickelgren, 1969). The term acoustic has been used hitherto to describe the confusion effect; Conrad employed the term because he found (Conrad and Hull, 1964) that the highly confusable sequences in the serial recall task were harder to discriminate in noise than the less confusable sequences. It is equally possible, however, that the coding may be articulatory in nature; that is, it may be derived from kinaesthetic movements in subvocal rehearsal of the letters. This hypothesis is supported by the detailed analysis of Hintzman (1967). He found that letters which employed the same articulatory apparatus were highly confusable, even though they were easily distinguished in noise. On the other hand, it has been shown that when subjects vocalize at presentation, the addition of white noise increases the number of confusions in recall (Murray, 1965). Moreover, if subjects put out their tongue and closed their teeth on it, thereby effectively preventing articulatory activity, the number of confusions was no greater than when they were permitted articulatory activity in silent reading (Gumenik, 1969). Thus the evidence points both ways.

A further ambiguity concerns the definition of articulatory coding. This may not be peripheral in nature only – the articulatory apparatus itself may not need to be activated. Rather, the central neural processes which regulate articulation may be activated without the musculature itself being affected (this assumption is the basis of the motor theory of speech perception, a currently influential position). Thus Hintzman's analysis in terms of the place of articulation does not necessarily imply that that place has to be physically activated. Rather, it may be the central processes which regulate that peripheral activity that are involved when the subject confuses two letters having the same place feature. Therefore the prevention of muscular articulatory activity is not synonymous with the prevention of articulatory coding; and its failure to increase confusions (Gumenik, 1969) does not argue against an articulatory hypothesis.

In the face of this conflicting evidence, it seems reasonable to suppose that both acoustic and articulatory coding may be involved. Levy (1971) showed that when overt articulatory coding is prevented, acoustic coding can compensate. For in a situation in which all subjects uttered 'hi-ya' after each letter was visually presented, subjects who heard the letter name through earphones performed better than subjects who did not. Since the benefit of hearing the letter was greater in this case than when subjects pronounced the letter normally, it was concluded that both acoustic and articulatory coding can be stored, and 'the loss of one type of information can be compensated for by use of the other, whichever is most task-relevant'. Once again, a question posed originally as an either-or is better viewed as a both-and, with relative proportions being task specific.

2.3.3 Acoustic coding to facilitate recall

Conrad's work and subsequent experiments used experimental techniques in which acoustic coding was evidenced by the *interference* effects of acoustic similarity. There are other tasks, however, in which acoustic coding may be employed to facilitate recall.

For example, Bruce and Crowley (1972) report an experiment in which four acoustically similar words were presented as part of a list of thirty-two words in a free-recall task in which there was a delay of thirty seconds between presentation and recall. The four items were presented either randomly distributed throughout the list, or blocked together. They were recalled better than four acoustically dissimilar control words, but only in the blocked presentation. This implies that acoustic coding only occurred when the acoustically related items were processed consecutively. Perhaps this was because the acoustic features common to the four items were only perceived in this condition; or perhaps it was because the items needed to be rehearsed together before they could be stored by a common acoustic code. However, the fact remains that acoustic features may be used in aiding memory (see also Craik and Levy, 1968).

A very different technique will serve as another example of the facilitatory effect of acoustic coding in a long-term memory task. Nelson and Rothbart (1972) had subjects learn twenty-four paired-associates (see 3.1.1), with the stimulus term being a number, and the response term a word. Four weeks later they were tested for retention of this learning, and were then set to relearn the associations. During this relearning, some response items were changed, while others remained the same. The difference between the number of trials required to relearn the unchanged items and the number required to relearn the changed items is an index of the amount of savings from the original learning. These savings can be calculated in particular for the items that were forgotten over the four-week retention period. It has been shown that even when items have been forgotten, there is still this savings effect — they are learned quicker than different response items. However, it is important to ask what it is that is saved. Some part of the coding of the originally learned response must have been available. Nelson and Rothbart indicate that at least part of the coding must have been acoustic in nature. For they compared relearning of the original stimulus-response term with homophones of the original response term. These homophones were either visually similar to the original response term (prey, pray) or visually dissimilar (whale, wail). It did not make any difference: in both cases, savings were far greater than in a condition where words unrelated to the original response term were 'relearned'. In other words, the original learning must have employed acoustic coding.

The importance of these results is not only that they

demonstrate the existence of acoustic coding; it is also that they show its effectiveness even after a considerable presentation-recall interval. As will be argued later (7.2.2), this effectively destroys any attempt to limit the scope of acoustic coding to so-called primary memory.

However, it must be admitted that most of the evidence of acoustic coding is in tasks with short retention interval, rapid presentation, and not very meaningful material (Underwood, 1969). Acoustic coding suffers from not having a rich bundle of attributes; if only one of the features of the letter P is lost, it may be recalled as B. However, since this sort of coding is quick to apply, it is useful when items are presented very rapidly. Furthermore, it is in a form which is amenable to rehearsal. Therefore it is useful for certain tasks which require rehearsal.

2.4 The modality effect

2.4.1 Auditory superiority
Several of those forms of registration and coding which have been described in sections 2.1, 2.2 and 2.3 have been used to attempt to explain a very well-attested finding. It has been found in a wide variety of recall and recognition tasks which follow closely after presentation that auditory presentation of verbal items results in superior performance to visual presentation (Murdock, 1972). This superiority has in most cases been limited to the last few items presented. Where the latter items of a sequence are better recalled than other items, this is known as the *recency* effect, since the last items in the list are those most recently presented; where the earlier presented items are better recalled, it is termed a *primacy* effect. Auditory superiority has been evidenced in the recency effect or in an overall superiority over the whole list.

Various techniques have shown auditory superiority. The most frequently used has been the probe technique. Essentially, this involves the experimenter reproducing at the time of test one of the items (the probe) which had previously been presented in a sequence of items. The subject's task is to state which item followed the probe in the presentation sequence; this is a probed recall task. Or he may simply have to state whether the probe item did occur in the presentation sequence or not (probed recognition task). Clearly, since the probe item can be derived from any position in the presentation sequence, the subject's recognition or recall of items from different parts of the sequence may be compared. Murdock (1967) found either overall or recency superiority for auditory presentation using a recall probe task, and overall superiority using a recognition probe (Murdock, 1968).

A second technique has been the *serial recall* procedure. Items are presented in a sequence, and the subject's task is to recall them in the same sequence. Here again, a recency effect has been found, with auditory proving superior to visual presentation over the last few items only. In most cases, the superiority is evidenced over the last three items only (e.g. Conrad and Hull, 1968), but there is some evidence of a more extensive effect (e.g. Madigan, 1971).

Free-recall performance also evidences a superiority for auditory over visual presentation (Murdock and Walker, 1969). When modality is varied between lists (that is, when one list is completely auditory, another completely visual) the superiority is evidenced only in a recency effect. However, when modality is varied within lists, so that some items are auditory, others visual, then the auditory superiority is over all the list.

2.4.2 Explanations of the modality effect
There are certain further results which narrow down the range of possible alternative explanations for the modality effect. The distractor technique has proved particularly useful in this respect. This technique requires the subject to engage in a distracting task between presentation and recall. The function of this task has usually been to prevent rehearsal of the presented items, not to interfere actively with them. Therefore the task has usually consisted of unrelated material to the presented material. Thus, for example, if the presented material were words or nonsense syllables, the distractor task might be to count backwards in threes from a three-figure number. However, in the area of modality effects, manipulation of the distractor task has resulted in differential effects on auditory superiority. When the distractor task is shorter, for example, auditory superiority is greater; this is also true when the distractor task is manual rather than verbal (Tell, 1971). From these findings it may be inferred that auditory superiority is unlikely to be located at the registration phase of information processing; for the distractor

task operates on the material *after* it has been coded. Therefore any effect of the nature of the distractor upon recall must be attributed to its interfering with the retention of coded material. The fact that a verbal distractor resulted in a decrease in the auditory superiority implies that the codings were verbal in nature; and the effect of the length of the distractor task implies that they are fairly easily lost.

A second piece of evidence supports the suggestion that although the codings of items may be fairly short lived, they are unlikely to be precategorical (see 2.1.2). Craik (1972) showed that when covert rehearsal was permitted (by leaving the presentation-recall interval unfilled by a distractor task) there was an equal degree of auditory superiority to situations where there was no interval. In other words, auditory superiority can occur when *all* items have been coded into names (since rehearsal requires such coding). Moreover, the auditory superiority is just as pronounced when the items are three-syllable words than when they are one-syllable words (Watkins, 1972). If the modality effect occurred at a precategorical stage, then one would expect the superiority to be less for three-syllable words. For these would occupy more registration 'space' than one-syllable words, since they are not yet encoded into single units, viz., words. The absence of any difference suggests that they have been coded by the time the modality effect operates.

A final important additional piece of evidence concerns the rate of presentation. The faster the rate of presentation, the greater the superiority of auditory over visual (Murdock and Walker, 1969). The finding implies that coding of visually presented items takes longer, and that when adequate opportunity for such coding is provided, the auditory superiority decreases.

Laughery (1969) supposes that verbal material, whether presented visually or auditorily, is encoded verbally in a memory task. Posner (2.2.3, 2.2.4, 2.2.5) has shown that visual encoding *can* also occur, so it is not correct to assume that visually presented verbal material is *only* encoded verbally. However, it is reasonable to suppose that Laughery's assumption is in general justified. We may then infer that visually presented items take longer to encode than do auditorily presented items because more transformations are required. Therefore when items are presented at a rapid rate, more auditorily presented items can be encoded than visually presented items.

But if this ease of encoding theory is true, why should the effect be on the last few items of the list only? And why should auditory superiority still be evidenced even when the presentation rate is slow (Murdock, 1972)? One tempting alternative explanation is to suppose that there is an additional source of items for recall with auditory presentation, viz., the precategorical acoustic store (Craik, 1969). There would not be the same possibility of using the visual iconic store to supplement the coded material since this fades more rapidly. Apart from the objections outlined above, such an explanation would require precategorical acoustic storage to be credited with far longer duration (e.g. twelve seconds) than has been evidenced by the use of the suffix technique (e.g. two seconds). It would also require items to remain in precategorical acoustic store even though several items had entered it subsequently, equally at variance with Morton and Crowder's findings.

A third major alternative explanation is Murdock's (1967) theory of modality-specific stores. He suggests that material is retained in a specifically auditory or a specifically visual store. This occurs before it is coded into words. The auditory superiority occurs because the auditory store has a greater capacity than the visual. However, it has been shown above that there is evidence that after the material has been coded verbally, the auditory superiority is still present. Moreover, the evidence on which Murdock places most weight is open to a rather different interpretation. Murdock and Walker (1969) had presented mixed auditory and visual unrelated items in lists in a free-recall procedure. They found that subjects clustered together in recall visual or auditory items. They inferred that retrieval was from separate stores, but an equally valid interpretation is that retrieval was from a unitary store by means of modality codings (see 2.5.1). That is, subjects coded the unrelated items in terms of the most obvious attribute which differentiated some of them from others, viz., the modality of their presentation. The next section will deal in detail with many such episodic features of the experimental situation which subjects may use for coding purposes.

In summary, the reasons for auditory superiority are far from clear; but the explanation which would best fit the theme of this book is the first suggested: that auditory presentation of verbal material results in less coding being necessary than visual presentation. All that can be said is that this explanation is as reasonable as any other.

2.5 Coding derived from the experimental episode

2.5.1 Modality of presentation

Coding has so far been conceived of as the transformation by the subject of the material presented into a different form. He may derive attributes from the material as presented (Underwood, 1969), or he may completely change it to fit with already existing memories (Bower, 1972). This section is concerned with coding by means of attributes derived, not from the material *per se*, but from the specific episode in which it was presented (Tulving, 1972). In other words, the attributes are not inherent in the material; they are not, for example, concerned with the sound or meaning of presented words. Rather, they are derived from the event of presentation, and would include such features as which word preceded which on that occasion.

It was seen in 2.4.2 that unrelated items presented in a free-recall procedure were recalled in a grouped order; the items which had been presented auditorily were grouped together, and so were those which were presented visually. Subjects organized their recall in terms of the modality in which the items were presented, and therefore they used that attribute in coding them.

Hintzman, Block and Inskeep (1972) have provided further evidence about this sort of coding. Subjects were given standard free-recall instructions before being presented with lists of unrelated words. Within each list, one half of the words, randomly distributed, were presented auditorily, and the other half visually. Subjects recalled each of eight lists of words after it had been presented, being allowed three minutes for recall. Then, after all the lists had been presented and recalled, they were unexpectedly given a recognition test. They had to decide whether an item which the experimenter then provided had occurred or not, and whether, if it had, its presentation had been auditory or visual. The recognition test item itself was presented either in visual or in auditory form.

Thus there was a situation in which subjects did not know that they were going to have to retain information about modality. However, they were found to be capable of retrieving such information when subsequently required to do so. Furthermore, this retention was for periods of several minutes, since there was a considerable interval between presentation of the earlier lists and the recognition test. The same results were obtained when the criterion feature was whether the voice uttering the items was male or female (with auditory presentation throughout); and when it was whether the items were printed in capitals or lower-case letters (with visual presentation throughout). Not only could subjects recognize items according to these features; they also recalled items clustered by them.

However, it still remains to be discovered how such information is retained. One suggestion is that its modality of presentation is encoded as an abstract attribute of each word. This implies that the modality attribute is abstracted from the presentation situation, and is represented abstractly and conceptually (though not necessarily verbally) in memory.

It is possible that attributes of this sort, derived from the experimental situation, act not as separate attributes, but in combination. Hintzman (cited in Posner and Warren, 1972) found that in cases where subjects could not remember which of two repetitions of an item had been auditory and which visual, they were able to do so when the experimenter placed each repetition in the position it had occupied in the presentation list. This implies that subjects coded items in terms of both modality and position, and that these two attributes interacted in the retrieval of modality information. Perhaps, however, one should not be surprised at this finding. For if an item is to be coded by means of attributes, and if the coding is to discriminate the item adequately from other items, then several attributes will have to be extracted. As Underwood (1969, p. 559) says, 'When a memory is conceptualized as consisting of an ensemble of attributes, memory for an event *per se* has no psychological meaning, because a memory without attributes is incapable of being retrieved.' Thus one cannot conceive of the item as presented being stored with a set of attributes or tags; rather, what is stored is a set of attributes from which the item may be reconstructed when required. Therefore it is obvious that attributes will interact to decrease uncertainty as to the nature of the item. They may not only act additively, but also multiplicatively; thus suppose the item to be coded is a person's name and suppose one codes it in terms of its initial letter, and in terms of the area of psychology in which that person works, then uncertainty is reduced more by these attributes in combination than it is by the sum of their separate effects.

2.5.2 Order

Hintzman (1970) and Hintzman and Block (1971) have used the same technique to show that other attributes of the presentation situation are also encoded. The position of an item in the list, the number of times an item is repeated within a list, or even the number of other items between two repetitions of an item can be reported by subjects, who, it must be stressed, were only given very general instructions at presentation. Underwood (1969) reports an experiment in which he shows that subjects do not necessarily remember the order of those items they recall, and vice versa. Memory for order cannot therefore be explained in terms of any simple strength hypothesis, where the order information would be derived directly from the strength of the 'trace' of the item itself.

However, most of the research on attributes such as order of items has employed the serial-recall task. It is reviewed by Estes (1972), and uses the same basic technique as the work on acoustic confusions (2.3.1). Briefly, the experimental situation is as follows. A set of four letters is presented visually and sequentially at a fast rate (e.g. 2.5 per second) to subjects. They have to read these aloud. They then have to read aloud a set of digits at the same rate. Finally, they have to recall the letters in the same order as they were presented. Experimenters seek to distinguish item and order properties in recall, treating certain errors as indicative of the loss of order information. These errors are where a letter which was presented at a particular position has been replaced in the subject's recall by a letter which had appeared at presentation in some other position in the same sequence.

Estes (1972) characterizes the overall results in this area as demonstrating (a) high accuracy of recall for order, (b) differences in the rates at which order and item information are lost, (c) differences in the positions in the sequence at which order and item information are lost, and (d) effects concerning grouping. Clearly, order properties are distinct from item properties, and order information is coded very effectively.

The grouping effects are particularly important if any theoretical account is to be given of how subjects code order information. Wickelgren (1967) made subjects group items within strings of eight, nine or ten digits into units of from one to five digits. The size of these chunks did not affect the number of items recalled to any significant extent, but it did affect the probability that a digit from a string was recalled in the correct position if it was recalled at all. This probability reached its maximum when there were three items per chunk. Wickelgren (1969a) found that if one item within a chunk was correctly recalled, the next was highly likely to be correct also. However, there was a much higher probability of a transitional error if the next item was the beginning of a new chunk.

The implication of this work on grouping is that chunks are coded, and that the code of a chunk contains the order and item information relating to the member items. It appears to rule out any attempt to use sequential cueing as an explanatory device. This would suggest that the first item cues the second, the second the third, etc. That subjects *can* employ a sequential cueing device is clear from the results of probe experiments which ask for the recall of the item which succeeded the probe item in the presentation sequence (Wallace, 1970). But the results of the grouping experiments indicate that there may be hierarchical as well as sequential modes of coding order.

Indeed, there is one finding of N. F. Johnson's (1970) which suggests that sequential coding plays little part even within chunks. Johnson presented interfering material to subjects in between the presentation of chunks and their recall. This material consisted of the to-be-recalled chunk with one of its three letters changed. It made no difference which one of the letters was changed, the first, second or third. All had equally deleterious effects on the recall of the other letters in the chunk. If there were sequential cueing within each chunk, altering the first letter should have the most deleterious effect. For that would prevent the second letter being cued, and hence the third.

However, this approach still fails to specify *how* order information is coded. It merely suggests that coding of the order of a whole list is more hierarchical then sequential. But the form in which the order information is coded may be in terms of position tags. That is, the subject may assign an abstract representation of where the item is within a chunk to each item. This representation need not be in the form of a number (the seventh item). It might instead be represented spatially, with the items coded as a linear series. Perhaps these series need to be short — this would explain why order information is best when chunks are of three items. There is some evidence to show that subjects do have available ordered list structures which function as whole units. For example, when subjects are given a recognition task, the object of which is to state whether or not a probe digit was one of the set 3456, their search rate through the series is not uniform. Rather, the nearer the middle of the set the probe digit is, the quicker the positive recognition response (Morin, De Rosa and Stultz, 1967). This implies that the set is treated as a spatially integrated unit. Underwood (1969) quotes other studies in which the spatial features of the presentation situation are coded, e.g. when different items are presented in different positions. But these are highly speculative suggestions.

2.5.3 Time

There are, however, other attributes of the presentation situation which might give additional information about order. One of these is the attribute of time. If one item was presented prior to another, then at least the order of those two items relative to each other will be retained if each is coded by its temporal attribute (i.e. how long ago it was presented). Clearly, however, for the temporal attribute to be the sole clue to order, every item would have to be coded by its time attribute. This would add to the number of attributes for each item coding; it would probably also throw an impossible load on the temporal judgement of the subject, since he would have to make fine judgements about immediately consecutive items.

One sort of evidence about temporal coding derives from experiments in which subjects indicate *to which of two presentation lists* an item belonged (Winograd, 1968). Since one list is presented before another, then ability to state to which list an item belonged may depend on a time judgement. On the other hand, many other features of the list situation may also be used to differentiate list membership. For example, in Winograd's experiment, the two lists were presented either the same number of times or different numbers of times respectively. Subsequent recognition of which list an item had belonged to was better when the lists had been presented different numbers of times. Bower (1972) suggests that this is because the discrimination between lists is itself coded by as many different attributes as are available, and in this case, frequency of presentation is just such a discriminative attribute. The contrary effect is predicted and obtained when the lists *share* common attributes which do not discriminate between them. Thus if the same words occur in both lists, the lists share identical features, which makes them harder to discriminate (Hintzman and Block, 1971; Anderson and Bower, 1972).

As Bower (1972a) remarks, the concept of a list of items is an arbitrary one. The only real connection with the temporal attribute is that lists of items are usually presented sequentially over time. However, in principle there is no reason why two lists of items should not be presented visually and simultaneously. In this case it would become clear that a list may be defined as 'a collection of items that share an association to a distinguishing cue, or marker'. This marker (attribute) need not be temporal — it could be positional, e.g. that collection of items presented on the left-hand side of the sheet in a column.

A more effective method of showing that subjects can use temporal codings is that of *judgements of recency*. Essentially the subject's task here is to state how many other items have intervened between the first occurrence of an item in a sequence and its repetition (Hinrichs, 1970). Alternatively, he may be presented with two items which have been presented earlier in the list, and required to state which of the two occurred more recently (Yntema and Trask, 1963). Subjects are remarkably successful at both of these tasks. However, once again the difficulty lies in isolating temporal variables from other factors. For example, Yntema and Trask found that the shorter the interval between the occurrence of an item and the subject's recency judgement, the more accurate that judgement was. In other words, information about relative occurrence in time may be quickly lost over time. This could mean that the time information is closely connected with the other attributes of the item in memory. Moreover, when an item recurs several times in the list it is more likely to be judged more recent than when it does not recur (Morton, 1968), supporting this idea that temporal judgement is intimately tied in with the strength of the coding of the item.

2.5.4 Frequency

Another feature of item presentation which subjects use to code items is the frequency with which they have occurred in the list. Subjects are very good at informing the experimenter of the number of repetitions of an item. However, exactly the same difficulty is present in the investigation of this form of coding, as has been found in sections 2.5.1, 2.5.2 and 2.5.3. This is that, in order to demonstrate the existence of coding by frequency, one has to hold constant the strength and extent of all the other attributes of the coding of the item in question. But if coding by frequency *is* one of the attributes by which an item is coded, then varying the frequency attribute will result in overall variation also in the strength and extent of coding.

Underwood (1969) and Underwood and Ekstrand (1968) tried to solve this problem by showing that judgements of frequency were equally accurate when success of recall of the same item varied. Thus Underwood, for example, presented items one, two, three or four times in a sequence. The subject's task was to state subsequently (and without previously knowing that he would have to do so) the number of times a word had occurred. In the cases where the word had occurred two, three or four times, the subject might retrieve the number of occurrences better because the item had been encoded better as a result of its multiple presentation. However, in the cases where the item had occurred only once, strength of encoding and judgements of frequency were distinguishable. Single items which occurred early or late in the list were recalled better than items in the middle (primacy and recency effects). However, subjects were equally successful in saying that an item had occurred only once *wherever* in the list it had been presented. As Underwood remarks, 'if recall is used as an index of strength, and if the frequency attribute reflects only strength, the frequency judgements should have been higher for the words occurring at the beginning and end of the list than for those occurring in the body of the list'. However, as Underwood also remarks, 'to be convincing, evidence on the converse case should be available; that is, evidence showing that differential frequency was correctly perceived but where recall or strength was equivalent'. Underwood, Zimmerman and Freund (1971) have gone some way to providing this information. They have shown that subjects are equally good at retrieving information concerning frequency of occurrence within the list of items which differ in their overall frequency within the rest of the subject's experience.

2.5.5 Conclusions

The episode of presentation is a source of attributes by which items may be encoded. It has been made clear that such attributes as frequency, order and time are difficult to distinguish in their effects, both from each other and from other coding attributes. The success of researchers in demonstrating their use, however, makes one wonder how many more features of the situation subjects employ. Clearly, there are many potential features in the experimental situation which might either act as attributes for coding themselves, or might result in the selection of some attributes rather than others. Bower (1972a, pp. 92-3) prefers the notion of *context*, defined as 'the background external and interoceptive stimulation prevailing during presentation of the phasic experimental stimuli. Included here would be internal factors like posture, temperature, room and apparatus cues, and stray noises, as well as internal physiological stimuli such as a dry throat, pounding heartbeat, stomach gurgles, nausea, and boredom. But more significant than any of these is what the subject is thinking about, what his mental set is, at the time the experimental stimulus intrudes.' Bower mentions such features as the subject's internal monologue, his conceptions of and associations to the instructions, the task, his own strategies, the experimenter and his purpose, etc. He supposes that changes in these contextual features will result in the use of different attributes for encoding. For example, if the subject is very hot and thirsty, he is apt to encode the item 'water' by means of different affective dimensions and different associates from those he would employ if he were cool and the weather rainy. If he guesses that the experimenter is going to ask him to recognize the material, he may code it by different attributes from those he would use if he thought he was going to have to recall it (see Frost, 1971).

The findings of the present section (2.5) might suggest that codings are multiple in number and changeable in nature. These questions will be discussed at length later (4.1 and 4.3). But one question is worth asking now. Does it necessarily follow from a successful retrieval of a piece of information (e.g. which list an item was in) that the item was *coded* partly by the attribute of, e.g., list membership? If Underwood's (1969) account is accepted, subjects could code an item and its presentation situation by a few attributes, then reconstruct them from those attributes when recall is required. The list membership feature could be part of the reconstructed situation; but it need not have been part of the code. The subject who successfully recalls list membership may have inferred it from his coding during the process of reconstruction.

Chapter 2 as a whole will be summarized at the end of Chapter 3.

Deeper forms of coding

3.1 Aspects of meaning

3.1.1 Natural language mediators

Sections 2.2, 2.3 and 2.4 presented data which suggested that visually presented verbal material, once registered, might be coded both visually and verbally. That is, subjects might have available different forms of coding simultaneously (Posner). However, it was argued that where verbal material was presented, subjects were likely to name the items; given a written letter, they were apt to code that letter by its name, and likewise for words (although not to the exclusion of visual coding). But the application of a name to the item by the subject is likely to be accompanied by the application of other additional attributes. This is also true when verbal items are presented auditorily and subjects code them by their names. These other attributes are derived from the subject's prior linguistic experience, not from the experimental situation. In the following sections, 3.1 and 3.2, the use of different features of the subject's linguistic knowledge for coding purposes will be reviewed. The emphasis here will be on the coding process; in Chapter 6 the structure of knowledge which makes such coding possible will be discussed. The function of this type of coding is usually elaborative. That is, the functional stimulus may consist of several attributes, the purpose of which is to enable the subject to discriminate the nominal stimulus from related stimuli. Retrieval of the correct item or event is thus ensured. The coding is multiple and rich, making use of the well-learned but complex linguistic structures available to the subject.

One such use will now be described. The technique employed in the investigation of *natural language mediators* (NLMs) (see Prytulak, 1971, for a review) has usually been paired-associate learning. This technique was originally devised to investigate how subjects acquired the associative connection between a stimulus and a response term. The aim was to eliminate prior learning as a confounding factor by using nonsense syllables, presumed to be novel items in the subjects' experience. However, it was soon found that such control was impossible. Subjects coded the stimulus as presented by using various aspects of their linguistic repertoire. Thus it was found, for example, that some nonsense syllables were more meaningful than others, in the sense that they elicited more word associates in a period permitted for free association. The way in which the subject coded the stimulus term was called a mediating response.

The technique of paired-associate learning requires the experimenter to present on the first learning trial a set of pairs of items (e.g. nonsense syllables, words). On the second and subsequent trials, the first item of the pair only (the stimulus term) is presented. The subject has to recall the response term. After a short period, the response term is presented. Then both stimulus and response terms are removed, and the next stimulus term is presented. The usual measure of learning employed is the number of trials required to reach a criterion of completely successful responding.

If the stimulus term is coded, then the mediating response will facilitate the learning of the association if it has connections also with the response term. Thus if the stimulus term is 'soldier', and the response term 'navy', then the mediating response 'sailor' to the stimulus 'soldier' will facilitate learning of the association; for 'sailor' is also closely associated with 'navy' (Russell and Storms, 1955). Such mediating responses are supplied by the linguistic system of the subject, for he is coding the stimulus term by the words to which it is closely related. This has been termed 'natural language mediation' (NLM).

Within the general paradigm of paired-associate learning, the first method employed in the investigation of NLMs (Adams and Montague, 1967) required subjects to report whether or not they had employed mediators after they had completed a paired-associate learning task. They claimed to have used mediators for two-thirds of the word pairs. The remaining third were assumed to have been learned by rote (but see Prytulak, 1971). Of the mediators reported, the greater proportion consisted of sentences. For example, if the word pair presented had been 'inshore-victor', subjects reported 'I thought of troops landing on a shore'. The next most common mediator reported was a single word, e.g. for the word pair 'retail-wealthy', a subject reported the mediator 'money'. Those pairs for which the subject reported providing a mediator were better recalled in a subsequent free-recall test than those for which he did not. Moreover, they were less liable to interference by a second list in which the same stimulus terms were learned with different response terms (see also Groninger, 1966).

Unfortunately, there is a basic difficulty in the method used in these experiments. It is possible that the reported mediators were not actually used to chain stimulus to response terms, but were added after the basic association had been formed. A second method which partly obviates this difficulty is to tell subjects to produce NLMs after each pair of items is presentéd. Montague, Adams and Kiess (1966) used this method in a modified paired-associate task. Subjects were presented with a pair of nonsense syllables, then asked to write down any NLMs they had. The recall task was to write down both the NLM (if any) and the response term, given the stimulus term. Results showed that it was only when the NLMs were successfully recalled in the form in which they were applied at presentation that their presence facilitated recall.

However, on the majority of occasions, the NLMs were forgotten. Moreover, in another experiment using the typical paired-associate task (Adams and McIntyre, 1967), the number of NLMs reported actually decreases on later trials. If they are acting as mediators, then they should increase over trials as the association becomes better learned (Underwood, 1972). One explanation (Prytulak, 1971) is that the nonsense syllables become coded into meaningful words, so mediators would be less necessary.

It must be concluded that the extent of the use of NLMs has not been established, nor has an adequate explanation been proposed for their effects on performance. Moreover, they appear to be consciously applied and somewhat artificial codes.

They do not often appear to tap linguistic skills in any direct way, but rather seem to have the function of coding unfamiliar material into a more meaningful form. In other words, the term *mediation* is probably not justified — it has not been established that the NLM serves to code the association between the stimulus and response terms. Moreover, the term *language* is also unjustified. For example, although the subject reports a mediator, 'troops landing on a shore', the report is verbal but the coding itself need not be. It could, for example, be a visual image. Thus NLMs reemble the Holy Roman Empire, neither Holy, nor Roman, nor Empire.

3.1.2 Connotative features
Osgood, Suci and Tannenbaum (1957) provided evidence that when subjects rate the affective (connotative) meaning of words, they do so along three basic dimensions. These they termed evaluative, potency, and activity dimensions. They argued that any word had a value on each of these dimensions for each individual, and, therefore, that it could be defined in terms of its position in the 'semantic space' defined by the dimensions. Clearly this is an early example of the approach recommended by Underwood (1969). Words may be coded in terms of attributes, which define the word in sufficient detail for it to be subsequently reconstructed. However, it is also evident that the affective meaning is but one of many possible attributes by which a word may be coded; it is unlikely that a subject could retrieve a word at recall on the basis of its affective meaning alone.

Instead of reviewing the great deal of experimental work which has employed the Semantic Differential rating scale as a tool, this section will deal with one particular experimental technique. A general review of the former may be found in Pollio (1968). The specific technique to be described is that of *release from proactive inhibition* (PI) (Wickens, 1970, 1972). It is selected for particular attention because it has implications for theoretical questions; it sheds light on the problems of how many attributes are coded, and whether they exist independently of the word itself. It is selected because it shows by a traditional memory paradigm that connotative features are employed in coding for memory. And, finally, it represents another good example of how a research technique may be exploited thoroughly.

The history of the technique of release from PI is worth sketching briefly. Brown (1958) and Peterson and Peterson (1959) had invented a distractor technique whereby after the presentation of a single item, subjects counted backwards in threes during the presentation-recall interval. Their purpose had been to prevent rehearsal, and therefore supposedly to tap short-term memory store exclusively (see 7.1.2). However, Keppel and Underwood (1962) showed that if one repeated this procedure several times, with different single presentation items on each occasion, recall performance deteriorated over trials. In other words, items presented on earlier trials proactively inter-fered with items presented on later trials. This finding was used to argue against the concept of a short-term memory store in which the laws of interference so widely evidenced in long-term memory did not apply (see 7.1.1). Wickens introduced a crucial variant into the technique. He employed a similar procedure for the first three trials, permitting the build-up of PI. For example, he presented three words on the first trial, three different words on the second, and yet another three on the third. Recall performance deteriorated, with the last three words being recalled considerably worse than the first as a result of PI. Then, on a fourth trial, he changed the basis of the categorization for the experimental subjects. They were presented with three numbers. Typically, they recalled considerably more than a control group who had received numbers over all four trials. The same was true of the reverse change, from numbers to letters. This improvement is termed 'release from PI' and is attributed to changing the crucial attributes. The inference is that the items were coded by the attributes over the first three trials, and therefore it becomes more and more difficult to retrieve the *correct* items at recall, since many of the same attributes are used for all items. Therefore these attributes cannot be used to discriminate one item from the other successfully. However, the fourth list is coded by different attributes, and is not therefore subject to the same interference.

The technique is thus of use in discovering which are the attributes by which a word is coded. One of the major dimensions along which changes have resulted in release from PI is that of *connotative meaning*. Words selected from Semantic Differential ratings as being equal on two of the three dimensions (evaluative, potency, and activity) but either positive or negative on the third have resulted in release from PI. That is, if, for example, words of a positive evaluation are presented for the first three trials and words of a negative evaluation for the fourth, release from PI occurs. This is true for all three dimensions. It is worth noting, however, that it does not necessarily follow that only the affective dimension in question is employed for coding. Other attributes correlated with it may have been used by the subject unbeknown to the experimenter.

In a clever extension of the technique, Wickens and his colleagues presented on the fourth trial items which differed in two dimensions rather than one. The dimensions on which changes occurred were the evaluation and activity dimensions. When both these dimensions were shifted, release from PI was significantly greater than when either one was shifted alone. This implies that items were coded on more than one connotative dimension. There were exceptions, however. When the fourth trial consisted of items on the positive end of the evaluative dimension, there was no increase in degree of release from PI when these items were shifted on another dimension as well. This implies that there may be occasions when one dimension only is used for retrieval purposes.

When the release from PI technique was applied to the development of coding by connotative dimensions in children, it was found that the evaluative dimension was employed by 7-year-olds to a highly significant extent. However, the activity dimension was only applied to a non-significant extent by 11-year-olds, and the potency dimension not at all. It is only when subjects are college students that all three dimensions are coded. Thus it may be the case that the evaluative dimension is preferred for retrieval purposes in the multiple-dimension situation because it is earlier established developmentally.

The suggestion that subjects may code a visually presented item in terms of some of its attributes before they code it by its name is made by Wickens (1972). Such a finding would suggest that the coding of an item by its name is not a necessary condition of its being coded by other features; and perhaps, even, that the encoding of the attributes assists in the encoding by the name. Wickens has shown that the three connotative dimensions are among the attributes which may be identified very early after presentation. The experimental method was to present a word visually for a very brief period of time. This period was so brief as to prevent the identification of the word name (from fifty to eighty milliseconds). After this presentation, a visual noise backward-mask was presented for one and a half seconds. Then a word was presented for five seconds. Subjects were asked to judge whether this latter word had some similarity to the experience produced by the previous word. One half of the words presented second actually did share a common attribute with the target word. Subjects succeeded in making more successful judgements when the similarity concerned was a connotative dimension than would be expected on the basis of the success rate of control subjects. However, the effect did not obtain for all dimensions, but only for the positive and negative poles of the evaluative dimension, and the positive pole of the activity dimension. These were the dimensions which occurred earlier in the developmental sequence in children.

The release from PI technique has shown that connotative dimensions can be used by subjects to code words for memory, and that more than one dimension may be used at a time; the matching technique has indicated that connotative attributes may be applied before the subject names the stimulus presented; and both techniques suggest that the dimensions favoured for these purposes are those which are acquired earliest in development. Other implications of Wickens's work will be discussed in 3.1.3 and 4.1.1.

3.1.3 Denotative features

The distinction between connotative (emotional, affective) meaning and denotative (referential) meaning serves to distinguish areas of research. Nevertheless, it must be stressed that subjects may use many different features of the material in order to code; use of one type of feature does not imply non-use of another.

Linguists have provided many fruitful hypotheses about the nature and identity of the denotative features of language (Kintsch, 1972). Psychologists relying entirely on the notion of association (defined operationally as responses in the free association task) may be ignoring vital aspects of meaning. Responses in the free association task are primarily differentiated on the basis of strength. That is, the response 'white' may be a stronger (more frequently given) response to the stimulus 'black' than is the response 'yellow'. However, there are many other logically different types of semantic relationship between words.

For example, one can distinguish hyponymy (red—colour) where the second term is a superordinate of the first, antonomy (huge—tiny), converse (give—take), incompatibility (e.g. the set of numbers, or colours, where one member of the set cannot be identical with another), and other relations. Words *may* be related to each other, therefore, in a great many ways.

This is not meant to imply that words presented in a memory task are coded in terms of a large number of other words, which are either also among those presented or else in the subject's vocabulary. Firstly, such a form of coding has to be evidenced experimentally before we may assume that it is one among the many possible sources of features for coding. Secondly, it is unnecessary to assume that the denotative coding of a word in memory is in terms of other *words*. It may be in terms of features or attributes which the presented word shares with other words. The presented word may, for example, be coded by features of a more general class to which it belongs (e.g. the word 'dog' may be coded in terms of attributes of pets — animals kept in the house). It may be coded in terms of the features which define it as a dog (e.g. it barks). It may be coded in terms of the exemplars of dog (poodle, alsatian, etc.) (Rumelhart, Lindsay and Norman, 1972). Moreover, there is no reason to suppose that the features employed for coding are in any sense linguistic in form. As will be shown in 3.3 they may well be sensori-motor in origin.

Four different types of evidence will be cited which suggest that subjects code words presented in a memory task in terms of their denotative meaning. It will become clear, however, that these experiments seldom permit any inference about the nature of the coding. That is, they do not indicate whether the subject employs other *words* as coding attributes or whether he extracts *features* of denotative meaning.

The first type of evidence is provided by the *false recognition* data. Essentially, a list of items is presented to the subject, who is subsequently shown individual items and asked to say whether or not an individual item was one of those presented in the list. When a subject says that a subsequently presented word did occur in the list when it did not, false recognition has taken place. The experimenter selects the false items he presents according to certain criteria. Underwood (1965), for example, using a related technique, selected words which were common associates of the list words. The false item was more frequently falsely recognized when it was an associate than when it was a control word which was not an associate. This was true of different forms of associate, e.g. antonyms (bottom—top) and superordinates (elm—tree).

Anisfeld and Knapp (1968) showed that the same effect could be obtained when the false items were synonyms, not associates. They also showed that false recognition of associates occurred only when the test word was a frequent response term to the presentation list word. It did not occur when the list word was a frequent response to the test word. An example: if 'bitter' were the presentation list word, and 'sweet' the test word, then false recognition occurred. The association in this case is from 'bitter' to 'sweet', since in the free association norms 'bitter' commonly elicits 'sweet', but not vice versa. However, if 'light' were the list word and 'heavy' the test word, false recognition would not occur. This is because 'light' does not normally elicit 'heavy' as a free associate, although 'heavy' frequently elicits 'light'. Thus it is only when the presentation words are the stimulus term in the free association norms that the false recognition occurs. False recognition cannot therefore be an artefact of testing for it. In other words, the test item is not eliciting the presentation item as an associative response. The only alternative explanation for the false recognition is, therefore, that the presentation item actually elicited the test word or was coded by attributes it shared with the test word at presentation (see also Cramer, 1970).

More generally, Anisfeld and Knapp (1968) conclude that coding must be in terms of abstract attributes if both associates *and* synonyms produce false recognition. Kimble (1968) showed that perceptual adjectives representing associated sense impressions (e.g. mountain—high, glass—smooth) could also be falsely recognized. Kendler and Ward (1972) similarly found that members of the same category as the presentation word were more likely to be falsely recognized than unrelated words. From the wide variety of types of test word which have produced false recognition, one may conclude that coding is more likely to be in terms of attributes than in terms of actual words.

A second technique indicating that words are coded by their denotative features is a variant of the *incidental learning* paradigm (Hyde and Jenkins, 1969). Essentially, this technique requires the subject to be presented with a list of words upon which he is told to perform certain tasks (orienting tasks). When presentation is completed he is unexpectedly told to recall the words. Since he was not aware that he was going to have to recall the items, he is unlikely to have engaged in any strategies for aiding memory. Therefore the effectiveness of the different forms of coding required by the orienting task may be estimated and compared uncontaminated by conscious strategies. If the task requires the subject to code items by attributes, and if this task facilitates recall, then it may be inferred that the coding of items by their attributes in memory does occur.

This is exactly what has been found. In their most recent and sophisticated work, for example, Hyde and Jenkins (1973) found that two semantic orienting tasks facilitated recall in comparison to various non-semantic tasks. The semantic tasks were rating each of the words along the pleasant—unpleasant dimension, and rating them for frequency of usage. The non-semantic tasks included ticking off the letters C and G when they occurred in the presented words, naming the part of speech of a word, and selecting the sentence frame from two alternatives into which the stimulus word fitted better (this last task seems to involve semantic as well as syntactic coding, however). The semantic tasks resulted in better recall than the non-semantic tasks. Moreover, they resulted in equally as good or even better recall than a control condition in which no task was given and subjects were told at presentation that they were going to have to recall.

The importance of these results is that they show that coding by specifically semantic (as opposed to syntactic) attributes aids recall. Moreover, the list does not have to consist of associatively related items. Hyde and Jenkins (1973) found that non-associates also were better recalled after the semantic tasks (although the facilitation was not so great as that of related words). Clearly, the features in the experiment quoted are not specifically denotative. However, the method is in principle capable of isolating other forms of semantic coding. Already experiments have shown that finding adjectives to fit presented nouns and vice versa (Johnston and Jenkins, 1971), and ratings along the active—passive dimension (Hyde, 1973), can facilitate recall in comparison with phonological or grammatical forms of coding.

The third technique which shows that coding may be in terms of denotative features is the even more versatile *release from proactive inhibition* (PI) (see 3.1.2). Wickens (1972) reports data which suggest that items are coded by more than one denotative feature. Wickens and his colleagues first showed that the presentation on the fourth trial of the procedure of items which differed in their taxonomic category from the items presented on the first three trials resulted in release from PI. Category membership is thus a coding feature which results in release from PI. In a later study, he varied the relationship of the categories to each other. The releasing category might be semantically 'close' to the learning category (e.g. 'vegetables' to 'fruit') or less close (e.g. 'flowers' to 'fruit') or totally unrelated (e.g. 'professions' to 'fruit'). Degree of relatedness was determined by the subjects' sorting behaviour. Results showed that when fruit items were presented on the fourth trial, they secured different degrees of release from PI depending on the closeness of their relationship with the category presented on the first three trials. There was hardly any difference between the control condition ('fruits' on all four trials) and 'vegetables'. This suggests considerable overlap of features between 'fruit' and 'vegetables'; Wickens suggests the possibility that they may both be encoded by such attributes as non-human, or to eat, but may differ in terms of when in the meal they are eaten. 'Flowers' result in considerably more release from PI. They may differ from 'fruits' in more respects (e.g. they too are non-human, but are decorative rather than for eating). Finally, 'professions', which result in most release, are human activities, not non-human; they do not seem to overlap with 'fruit' in any attributes. Obviously, these are speculations. We do not know what features are used to code the categories; for example one might speculate that natural as opposed to man-made might characterize 'fruit', 'flowers' and 'vegetables'. Further, we do not know to what extent individuals may use idiosyncratic codings. However, the important feature of the experiment is that it shows different degrees of release from PI for different categories. This implies that it is not simply a matter of the releasing items being given a different superordinate label (e.g. 'fruit') from the label appropriate to the training items (e.g. 'flowers'). For, in this case, the difference in the coding should ensure the same release in all cases. Rather, the items are coded by the attributes which define the category. Once again, it must be stressed that these need not be verbal at all.

The final technique which has been heavily employed to

evidence denotative coding is cued *free recall*. The subject is provided with a cue by the experimenter, and the effectiveness of the cue in helping the subject to recall the items is taken as an index of the extent to which the subject coded the material in terms of the cue at presentation. Thus word codings of nonsense syllables (e.g. cage—CAG) have been successfully employed as cues (Lindley, 1965). So have weak associates of the to-be-recalled words (Tulving and Osler, 1968). However, many of these experiments have employed the cues at both presentation and recall. Thus their success could be attributed to the fact that the experimenter had constrained the subject to use the cue as a code at presentation. There is therefore little evidence that subjects do use this type of cue as a code, only that they can do so when required. One exception to this generalization is the work of Bahrick (1969). Using associates of the to-be-recalled word as cues *at recall only*, he found that strong associates aided recall more than weak associates. However, it is not clear from these results whether the items were coded by the subject at presentation by means of related words (associates) or attributes.

The coding of *several* items by means of shared attributes is termed organization, and will be discussed in Chapter 5. The use of classical conditioning techniques to investigate semantic generalization is not discussed here. Maltzman (1968) provides a review.

3.2 Linguistic structure

3.2.1 The nature of language

The items presented to subjects in the research described hitherto have been molecular rather than molar. Letters, digits, nonsense syllables, and words have formed the material. In most cases the items have been chosen in such a way that there are no relations between items in the list. The list is simply a sequence of items chosen at random from an ensemble. However, it has been shown that even in the case of such molecular items as these, subjects code by means of linguistic rules. For example, the confusions in the recall of letters (2.3.1) may be due to failure to use all the phonological distinctive features to code them (see 2.3.2).

Linguistic skills, however, are developed to cope with the task of communication. Communication involves the understanding and producing of speech, which may be seen as a multiply coded set of signals (Herriot, 1970; Slobin, 1971). There are phono-logical, grammatical and semantic codes, each of which operates according to certain rules. That is, there are certain structural regularities and combinations of elements which are predictable and permissible, and others which are not. One may say 'Punch hit Judy', but not 'Punch Judy hit'; 'during the day', but not 'during the stairs'. It is clear, however, that these regularities are not on the surface. They do not consist of particular sequences of *words* which are permissible and other sequences which are not. Rather, they consist of more abstract regularities; for example, inanimate nouns cannot perform actions — boys may eat cakes, but cakes cannot eat boys.

On the other hand, these more abstract representations are not only *restrictive*; they do not only imply that some combinations of elements are not permissible. They are also almost infinitely *productive*. That is, having generated sequences of abstract elements which are permissible (e.g. subject plus predicate, or modifier plus noun, or agent plus action) one can produce an immense number of different utterances all of which fit the acceptable sequence.

In such a multiply coded situation as communication, the task of the speaker is to encode his utterance in such a way that he provides enough cues for the listener to decode it. His task, in other words, is to reduce the uncertainty of the listener as to what it is he (the speaker) wishes him to think or do. The listener has to use his knowledge of the different types of coding to decode the utterance in the way intended. Both speaker and listener employ the rules of the language to enable them to perform adequately; the speaker's planning and the listener's construction of the message are based on common knowledge of regularities in the structure of the language.

An example: given only the alternative messages 'per*mit*' and '*per*mit', the listener may be in some doubt how to construe them, since his only cue is the phonological one of stress. If the utterances become 'a *per*mit' or 'per*mit* me', the grammatical rules that an indefinite article must qualify a noun, while an object pronoun must follow a verb, reduce the uncertainty considerably. 'Per*mit* me the pleasure' versus 'Grant me a *per*mit' adds semantic cues; one expects the collocation of 'per*mit*' with 'pleasure', and grant with '*per*mit'. The very fact that the listener perceives an ambiguity (e.g. in 'I like cooking apples') indicates coding in terms of structure.

Linguists (Lyon, 1968, Lyons and Wales, 1971) analyse the 'deep' or abstract rules which they suppose underly the 'surface' form of utterances. Their characterizations appear to be changing; more recently, they have stressed the functional rather than the structural aspects of these deep features of language. That is, they are concerned with the relation of the utterance to its non-linguistic context rather than with the utterance in isolation. However, there is some doubt as to the extent to which the linguists' descriptions of the deep structure and its transformation into utterances correspond to psychological processes (Greene, 1972). They are possibly different types of analysis. The linguist is concerned to characterize the individual's knowledge of the language abstractly, outside the constraints of time and the human information processing system. The psychologist is concerned to discover the structure of the individual's linguistic knowledge and the processes by which he uses it to speak and understand speech. More important, he is more than willing to entertain the possibility that the processes and structures underlying communicative behaviour may be no different from those regulating other complex behaviour.

Granted, however, that the primary function of speech is to communicate; and granted that communication is by means of utterances which are encoded and decoded by the use of relations between abstract features; then it should be hardly surprising that when subjects are given phrases, sentences or passages to *remember*, they use the same codes as they do to *understand* or *produce* them. For, given material which conforms to their linguistic expectations, they are likely to employ linguistic codes automatically and unconsciously. However, if the task is different from the usual communicative one of understanding an utterance, then they may employ the linguistic codes in different ways and in different proportions to those employed in normal communication. If, for example, the task is to recall sentences verbatim, the phonological and grammatical codes may play a more important role than in understanding and speaking. If, on the other hand, the task is to recall the gist of a lengthy passage, it may resemble the communicative behaviour of understanding and speaking far more closely. We should therefore predict that the nature of the task will determine which forms of coding are employed; and we should be suspicious of all arguments which propose that *the* form of coding is x rather than y.

Research into memory for linguistically structured material can be described in terms of a progression from a search for a specific form of coding through to a realization of the multiple alternatives available. It can also be characterized as a progression from hypotheses based on specific linguistic theories to a merging of linguistic and cognitive aspects of coding.

3.2.2 Surface grammatical structure

One strand of research shows that sentence material may be coded in terms of its surface grammatical structure. Linguists distinguish surface from deep structure, with surface structure being defined as the analysis of a sentence into its constituent grammatical parts. Thus, for example, a sentence would be divided into a subject and predicate. These in their turn might be subdivided into smaller units, until the grammatical constituents might be described as: definite article (The) + qualifier (tall) + noun (boy) + verb (save) + past tense inflexion (ed) + definite article (the) + adjective (drowning) + noun (woman) = 'The tall boy saved the drowning woman'. The linguist's grounds for this analysis arise from several techniques, most of them involving substitution. Native speakers of a language are asked to substitute other words for a particular word in a sentence; the grammatical function of the word is consequently inferred from the other words chosen.

Epstein (1961) showed that strings of nonsense words with a grammatical structure (e.g. 'The erenstany cates elendied the edom eptly with ledear and aris') were better recalled in a multi-trial free-recall procedure than in randomized order or without the function words and inflexions. Johnson (1968) carried the analysis into meaningful sentences. He found that errors in the recall of sentences followed certain grammatical patterns. Errors in such sentences as 'The tall boy saved the drowning woman' were more likely to occur at major breaks in the grammatical structure. Thus, given that 'boy' was correctly recalled, there was considerable probability that 'saved' would not be correctly recalled. This 'transitional error probability' was higher between 'boy' and 'saved' than between 'saved' and 'the'. And it was higher between 'saved' and 'the' than between 'drowning' and 'woman'. Johnson concluded that subjects code the presented sentence in terms of its grammatical structure. When the time comes for recall, they go through the grammatical process of reconstructing the sentence from the coding. This reconstruction follows the surface-structure constituent analysis. Thus the subject produces the sentence in the same way as the linguist analyses the constituent structure, proceeding from larger to smaller units. The smaller the tnit, the less uncertainty the subject has in decoding the sentence, since he has already recoded e.g. the phrase 'the drowning woman' of which 'drowning' is a part. The subject's task may perhaps be seen as one of remembering grammatical commitments (Yngve, 1960). That is, when he hears a grammatical subject presented, he has to retain it in memory until he hears what the predicate is if he is to code the sentence as a whole. When he recalls the sentence, he has to store the grammatical commitment to utter a predicate until he fulfils it; thus, for example, if he recalls 'The tall boy . . .', he has incurred a commitment to utter a predicate which has to be fulfilled. Both Johnson's and Yngve's hypotheses suppose that the linguistic grammatical analysis is an accurate representation of the coding process. Martin and Roberts (1966) provided further support when they showed that sentences of greater grammatical complexity as measured by a constituent analysis were better recalled than sentences of a lesser complexity but the same length.

However, it appears unlikely that a formal description of one aspect only of linguistic structure will adequately represent a psychological process. This is particularly true of coding in memory, where, judging from previously cited evidence, multiple coding by many different attributes occurs. More recent evidence suggests that subjects do not use the units prescribed by constituent analysis alone. They may segment the sentence into subjective units of their own (Martin, 1970). For example, the grammatical subject and main verb of a sentence may be placed together in a single unit; constituent analysis always places together the main verb with the object in a predicate unit. It has been shown that the length of the preceding or following phrase can determine where the subject makes a break. Such divisions of units are more likely to occur when the previous or subsequent phrases are longer than others (Martin, Kolodziej and Genay, 1971).

More important than these exceptions to the surface-structure rules, however, is the possibility that other variables were confounding results; alternative modes of coding may equally well explain results attributed to coding by grammatical surface structure. One such variable is lexical density, the ratio of function words (e.g. the, however) to content words (e.g. boy, rapid). When this variable is treated as dichotomous and varied orthogonally with grammatical complexity, recall varied as a result of lexical density but not of grammatical complexity (Perfetti, 1969). Those sentences with more content words were less well recalled. This suggests that even when the task is verbatim recall of individual sentences, features of meaning are involved.

3.2.3 Deep grammatical structure

A second tradition of research supposes that sentences are coded in terms of their deep rather than their surface grammatical structure. This tradition owes its inspiration to Chomsky's (1957, 1965) analyses of linguistic structure. It maintains that subjects decode sentences presented to them into their deep structure, and then recode them into their required spoken form at recall. Deep structure is distinguished from surface structure because there are many sentences which have identical surface structures but very different underlying structures. For example, the sentences 'John is easy to please' and 'John is eager to please' have the same surface structure but different underlying structures. In terms of the surface grammatical structure, 'John' is the subject in both cases, but 'he' is the logical object in the first case ('It is easy to please John') and the logical subject in the second ('John is anxiously hopping from foot to foot ingratiating himself'). Deep structure is usually taken to consist of a set of propositions which are presupposed by the sentence. Linguists suppose that various tranformational operations have to be performed upon the deep structure to generate a surface structure. In order, for example, for a question to be asked, among other requirements a 'wh' element often has to be inserted at the beginning of the sentence and the normal position of the auxiliary verb and the subject noun reversed e.g. '*What is the boy playing?*'

One psychological hypothesis is to suppose that subjects code a sentence in terms of its deep structure together with instructions to perform the appropriate transformations. The transformational model, in other words, is taken over into psychology wholesale. Early experiments showed that types of sentence which required more transformational operations were harder to remember than sentences which required less. Passive sentences, for example, were harder than actives (Mehler, 1963). Savin and Perchonock (1965) employed a clever technique aimed at showing the amount of 'storage space' taken up by the respective sentence types. The subjects' task was to recall as many digits as they could in addition to the sentence itself. Differences in the number of digits recalled with different sentence types suggested that they differed in respect of their codings. The inference drawn from these experiments was that subjects coded the sentence in terms of its deep structure together with tags, or instructions, as to which transformations to perform upon the deep structure in order to reconstruct the presented sentence. One direct implication of this interpretation is that subjects should be able to remember the grammatical type of the sentence in an incidental learning task. Bregman and Strasberg (1968) found that they often could do so; but when they failed on their first guess, they succeeded on the second more often than would be predicted on the basis of chance. The implication is that subjects are not remembering transformational tags in an all-or-none manner, but are reconstructing a probabilistic estimate of the transformational type from other sorts of coding.

More recently, however, research has suggested that it is not the number and complexity of transformations from deep to surface structure which determine ease of coding. Rather, it is the actual complexity of the deep structure itself. This is what one would expect if subjects code in terms of the meaningful relations underlying the sentence. Thus, for example, Rohrman (1968) found that subject nominalizations such as 'growling lions' are easier to recall than object nominalizations such as 'digging holes'. These phrases differ in degree of deep structure complexity, since 'growling lions' implies a simple proposition, 'lions growl', whereas 'digging holes' implies a more complex proposition, viz., 'someone digs holes'. However, other subject and object nominalizations such as 'performing artists' and 'performing miracles' did not differ in ease of recall. In this latter case, the underlying deep structure complexity does not differ: the verbs in both cases are transitive, and therefore the underlying propositions are 'artists perform something' and 'someone performs miracles'. The two phrases *do* differ in the number of transformations required from their deep to their surface form, however, so the inference is that it is complexity of deep structure, not transformational complexity, which determines ease of recall. However, Rohrman himself (1970) subsequently suggested that the psychological operations involved were not grammatical. Analysis revealed that the subject nominalizations were more likely to be animate nouns and intransitive verbs, and the object nominalizations inanimate nouns and transitive verbs. It could be that these lexical features rather than deep structure complexity determined ease of recall.

Unfortunately there seems to be some doubt about the actual methods of defining and generating sentences of varying deep and surface structure. As a result, recent experimenters (Bacharach and Kellas, 1971) have suggested that most previous research has confounded deep and surface structure variables. Moreover, it is quite clear that the specific features of the experimental task determine which of the several linguistic types of code available are employed by the subject. In general, those tasks which require the subject to pay attention to meaning (e.g. by asking not for verbatim but for gist recall), or which permit him to assume that meaning is as important as it usually is, result in the subject coding by the deep structure. This is because deep structure reveals the essential elements of meaning in a sentence, such as who is the actor, or what is the topic.

Just two examples will be given of experimental tasks which by their very nature encourage the use of surface and deep structure analysis respectively. The surface grammatical structure was found to be used for coding by Bacharach and Kellas (1971) and by Heisey and Duncan (1971). But this is hardly surprising since they presented several sentences of the same grammatical type together. Subjects were set to pay attention to grammatical form. The deep structure was used for coding in cases where connected discourse was presented to subjects (Sachs, 1967). The implication was that the meaning should be attended to.

Subsequently, Sachs presented sentences selected from the passage in a recognition task. Sentences were either exactly as in the passage, or differed slightly. These differences involved either a change of the surface structure or the deep structure. False recognition occurred far more frequently when the change was in the surface structure. Subjects had coded for meaning, and so did not retain such features as whether a sentence was active or passive. Indeed, Jarvella (1971) shows that subjects only retain verbatim the immediately preceding context when being presented with continuous discourse; and that they can only do so when this preceding phrase is part of the sentence which was interrupted. The inference is that subjects code discourse in terms of its meaning, retaining the exact form of words only in the sentence currently being coded. Indeed, when a passage is recalled as a whole, the actual number of words correctly recalled is minimal, although the meaning is well retained (Howe, 1970).

3.2.4 Reconstruction

The import of these findings, then, is that when they perceive the task as requiring coding in terms of meaning, subjects use all the meaning cues available to them in order to do so. The question remains as to *how* they employ their knowledge to code the material. A strictly linguistic hypothesis would suppose that the subject codes the surface grammatical structure into its deep structure components, then notes the meaning relations which these imply. For·example, given the sentence 'The doctor was treated by the patient', he would code into the grammatical deep structure, the patient as the actor and the doctor as the one acted upon. However, Herriot (1969) found that this was not the case. The passive sentence just quoted and its active form, 'The patient treated the doctor', did not differ in the amount of time required to name the actor and the one acted upon. Had they needed to be grammatically analysed down to deep structure, the passive should have taken longer. However, both these sentences took longer than the sentences 'The doctor treated the patient' and 'The patient was treated by the doctor' (which did not differ between themselves). The inference is that when there are strong expectations concerning the roles of the characters, these are used to assign deep structure. Detailed grammatical analysis is not necessary. When there were no such expectations (e.g. 'The sister was hated by her brother'), there *was* a difference between active and passive forms.

Thus the expectations of the subject may determine his coding of meaning. He may, in fact, actually draw inferences from the content of the presented material and thus code a meaning which is not there. Thus when he comes to recall, he will *reconstruct* from this coding a message which substantially adds to or changes the presented material, not only in form but also in meaning. In his classic experiments, Bartlett (1932) showed how English subjects coded Eskimo folktales with a strong super- natural content into a more rationalized form. More recently, Bransford and his associates have used a more controlled technique. They devised complex sentences which could be broken down into simpler propositions. For example, the sentence 'The arrogant attitude expressed in the speech led to immediate criticism', may be broken down into: 'The attitude was arrogant' (one proposition); 'The arrogant attitude was expressed in the speech' (two); 'The arrogant attitude expressed in the speech led to criticism' (three); and the fourth proposition, 'The criticism was immediate', completes the complex sentence (above). The task was to recognize whether or not a test sentence was among those presented and to state the degree of confidence one felt in doing so. The presented sentences contained parts of the complex sentences, either one, two, three or all of the four propositions. The recognition sentences likewise contained vary- ing parts or all of the complex sentences. It was found that subjects were more confident that the test items with more parts had been presented originally than they were that those with less parts had been presented. This was true whether the recognition sentences actually had been presented, or whether they consisted of those parts of the complex sentence which had not been presented. The implication is that subjects, when they coded, added to the sentences presented so as to complete the complex idea. This is true of abstract ideas of which an example is quoted above (Franks and Bransford, 1972) and of concrete ideas (Bransford and Franks, 1971).

Johnson, Bransford and Solomon (1973) carried the technique a step further. The test recognition sentence was actually the inference which could be drawn from one of two presentation passages but not from the other. Consider the passage: 'The river was narrow. A beaver hit the log that a turtle was sitting on, and the log flipped over from the shock. The turtle was very surprised by the event.' Subjects who had been presented with this sentence were apt to falsely recognize 'A beaver hit the log and knocked the turtle into the water' as having occurred in the passage. Other subjects who had been presented with exactly the same passage, except with the word 'beside' substituted for 'on' were less likely to make a false recognition. The former subjects clearly *inferred* that the turtle was knocked into the water.

Therefore it would seem that subjects sometimes do more than perform analyses on presented material to obtain the deep structure. Their coding may additionally involve the drawing of inferences from the presented material. Inferential reasoning processes have resulted in the elaborative coding of meaningful material in such a way that the meaning is not retained but added to in memory.

This section will conclude with a case study of a sequence of experiments which shows the potential fruitfulness and at the same time the difficulties of research into memory for linguistically structured material. The initial experiment in this sequence was that of Rohrman (1968) described in 3.2.3. It will be recalled that he found that phrases differing in deep structure complexity were recalled with differential success. This was followed shortly by an experiment by Paivio (1971a). He used exactly the same material plus some additional phrases, and found that rated imagery (see 3.3) predicted success of recall, whereas deep structure complexity did not. High imagery phrases such as 'dancing girls' or 'changing tyres' were better recalled than low imagery phrases such as 'editing books' or 'persisting doubts'. Finally, Danks and Sorce (1973) used a prompted (cued) recall task. The two factors varied were deep structure complexity of sentence and rated imagery of the word in the sentence used as the cue for recall. They found both main effects, and, more important, an interaction. Degree of deep structure complexity only had a significant effect when the prompt word was of low rated imagery. And rated imagery only had an effect when the deep structure was more complex. In sum, this sequence of experiments shows the danger in psycholinguistic research of ignoring possible confounding variables (Rohrman), and of assuming that *one* form of coding is the preferred one (Paivio); we arrive at the sensible conclusion that different forms of coding will be used depending on the task material (Danks and Sorce). The major task remains: to show precisely which task variables determine the form of coding employed, and to explain how and why these forms of coding are effective.

3.3 Imagery

3.3.1 Evidence of its use

It has been seen already (2.2.3) that visually presented verbal material may be retained in a visual as well as in a verbal form. Recently considerable attention has been given to the possibility that many verbal items may be coded by images. Words, phrases or sentences may be transformed into visual or other images. The transformation is thus one of kind: linguistic material which is essentially *sequential* in the way in which it is perceived and produced is transformed into a different form of representation essentially *simultaneous* in nature. Reviews of the recent research are provided by Paivio (1969, 1971a) and Bower (1970a).

Most of the initial research employed the paired-associate learning task (see 3.1.1). Paivio (1969) reasoned that 'concrete' words would be more likely to be coded by an image than 'abstract' words. This distinction is somewhat *ad hoc*, and relates to whether the word refers to a physical object, attribute or action, or whether it refers to a non-physical one (e.g. truth, verbal, prevaricating). However, that the distinction was justified was shown by the rating data collected by Paivio, Yuille and Madigan (1968). They found that words which we intuitively feel are concrete are in fact rated by subjects as more highly evocative of imagery than words we consider abstract.

Given, then, that concrete words are more likely to evoke images than abstract words, certain predictions follow for the paired-associate task. It might be supposed that an image would serve as a mediator between the stimulus and response pair. This image would be a compound of the images evoked by the stimulus and by the response term. However, the image elicited by the stimulus term should be the more important contributor; for in the paired-associate task it is the stimulus which is given to the subject on each trial. The overt stimulus therefore acts as a cue from which the combined image has to be constructed. Therefore that part of the combined image which it evokes will be a cue in its turn for the reconstruction of the combined image.

Once the combined image is reconstructed, the response term can be retrieved. This analysis leads to specific predictions, given the possibility of manipulating the image-evoking potential of word pairs. First, words of high imagery should result in faster learning than words of low imagery; second, when the stimulus word is of high imagery, this should result in faster learning than when the response term is of high imagery. These predictions were supported (Paivio, 1969). It may be objected that concrete nouns also evoke more verbal associates ('are more meaningful') than do abstract nouns. Therefore the results might be interpreted in terms of verbal rather than imagery mediation. However, when the two factors of 'meaningfulness' and imagery were varied independently, and even when they were covaried, the imagery results could not be attributed to verbal factors. Further, imagery was shown to be a more potent mediator than verbal association.

Additional manipulations within the paired-associate task have provided further evidence. Subjects report more imagery when the stimulus terms are concrete nouns, although the value of reports is dubious; Di Vesta, Ingersol and Sunshine (1971) showed that when imagery was tested by subjective report, it was heavily loaded on a social desirability factor as revealed by factor analysis. Instructions to use imagery as a mediator also improve learning, though in some cases no more than do instructions to use verbal mediators. Moreover, when actual objects or pictures are used as stimulus terms instead of words, learning is faster.

Moving away from the paired-associate task, concrete nouns are better recalled in a free-recall task than abstract nouns. It is possible, however, that their very 'picturability' acts as a supercoordinate coding by which concrete words may be organized and clustered in recall. This would explain the increased amount recalled. Objects and pictures are better recalled than words; Paivio explains this finding in terms of availability of codings. Pictures or objects may be coded very easily into images, since less transformations are involved than in coding a word into an image. They may also, of course, be coded verbally. Concrete words may be coded by imagery and verbally, but abstract words only verbally. On these assumptions, presentation of pictures should result in superior recall performance in all tasks *except* those in which a fast rate of presentation and ordered recall is required. In these latter cases, words should be better recalled; for it takes less time to read a visually presented word than it does to apply a name to a picture. This prediction was verified (Paivio, 1969). In all other cases, however, the multiple encoding made easier by pictures results in better recall, as predicted by Paivio's theory.

3.3.2 Explanations of its effectiveness

Given, however, that imagery does occur and is highly effective, the question still remains *why* this type of coding should be so effective (Tulving and Madigan, 1970). One answer may lie in the *simultaneous* nature of visual imagery. Within *one* image, one functional unit in memory, the relationship between two or more nominal stimuli may be represented. Experiments using three different techniques all point to this attribute of imagery as the crucial factor in its facilitatory effect. The first experiment (Wollen and Lowry, 1971) employs the paired-associate learning task again. In this research, however, the experimenters actually provided a picture as a visual mediator between the two nouns to be learned. They found that it was only when this picture expressed a relationship between the stimulus and response terms that learning was facilitated. For example, if the items were 'horse' and 'tree', the horse would be pictured standing under the tree.

The second technique (Bower and Reitman, 1972) employs a well known mnemonic device. Subjects are taught to learn a list of words by pairing each word with a number and a rhyming concrete 'peg' word. Thus the first word in the list would be learned by being associated with 'one is a bun', the second with 'two is a shoe', etc. The subject is instructed to visualize the list word in some relationship with the peg word. Thus suppose the first list word is 'axe'; the subject might visualize an axe being used to cut a currant bun. This has been found to be a very effective mnemonic device. However, if it is used on several successive lists, retroactive interference sets in. That is, subsequent lists are learned worse because the peg words are already associated with different items learned previously. Bower and Reitman showed, however, that this need not be the case. They instructed subjects to add the item from each current list to the composite picture formed from all previous lists. Thus, for example, suppose that the first word of the second list presented was 'butcher'. In this case the image of the axe chopping up the currant bun would be modified by the subject to include a butcher wielding the axe. As a result of these composite images, the interference effect was removed; recall at the end of the experimental session of all the lists was greater for these subjects receiving 'progressive elaboration' instruction than for a control group who formed a different image for each pairing of the peg word with the item word.

A final technique involves the use of imagery to code sentences (Begg and Paivio, 1969). Sentences imply relations between elements. Sachs (1967), it will be recalled (see 3.2.3), had shown that false recognition of sentences occurred when the meaning was essentially unchanged, but a change in form had occurred; for example, a synonym had been substituted for one of the original words. However, when the test sentence reversed the logical subject and object of the original sentence, for example, subjects did not mistake it for the original. Begg and Paivio found that these results held for concrete sentences with a strong imagery component, like those employed in Sachs's study. However, when abstract sentences were employed, the opposite was true: changes in wording were better recognized than changes in meaning. Begg and Paivio attribute this finding to the coding of concrete sentences into complex images; changes in meaning would be recognized because they would not tally with these complex images. Such coding would not occur, they supposed, in the case of abstract sentences, which would be coded in verbal form. However, it is possible that the abstract and concrete sentences differed in recognizability because they differed in comprehensibility (Johnson, Bransford, Nyberg and Cleary, 1972). The concrete sentences could have been easier and quicker to code, and therefore Paivio and Begg's result might be attributed to the fact that subjects had managed to code concrete sentences but not abstract ones. There need then be no implication that the coding is necessarily visual in nature. It seems likely that subjects *do* manage to code abstract phrases meaningfully given time, however; for synonyms of presented abstract words result in more false recognitions when they are test items than do antonyms (Goldfarb, Wirtz and Anisfeld, 1973).

In general, however, it seems clear that imagery provides a readily available representation for reconstruction purposes. By means of a complex image, subjects can retrieve several items by the spatial relationships they have imposed upon them. However, it seems mistaken to try to *contrast* imagery with other forms of coding as mutually exclusive alternatives. Deep structure or natural language mediators, for example, are not *incompatible* with imagery. On the contrary, it seems fairly plausible to hypothesize that the attributes by which subjects code the nominal stimulus may themselves be subject to coding. Thus it is possible to see imagery as one particular way of storing a certain set of attributes extracted from the nominal stimulus. If the stimulus is a sentence, the set of attributes extracted might include the deep structure meaning; one way of storing this meaning might be by imagery. Thus deep structure coding need not be mutually incompatible with imagery.

3.4 Reductive coding

3.4.1 Stimulus selection
Most of the forms of coding described in this chapter so far have seemed to have the function of facilitating retrieval. The nominal stimulus has been coded in terms of its attributes; and sufficient attributes have been coded for the item presented to be retrieved, rather than another related item from the subject's semantic memory. It has been shown that these attributes may be derived from several different sources. For example, the experimental situation may serve as an external source, the subject's linguistic knowledge as an internal one. However, their major function is to distinguish the item from other material. Their use emphasizes the richness of the human memory in two ways: the number of different sources of coding available, and the number of attributes that are actually used on any particular occasion.

However, there are some situations in which the use of a wide variety of different forms of coding is not so likely. This section will deal with two such situations. The first situation is when the material presented is of very low meaningfulness, and the form of coding is termed stimulus selection (Richardson, 1972). The paired-associate learning technique is once again employed, with the stimulus term consisting of a compound (e.g. triple-consonant nonsense syllable) of separate components (e.g. the individual consonants). First the paired-associate list is learned with the compound stimulus (e.g. RXQ) as the stimulus term. Then subsequently each consonant is presented as the stimulus term, and subjects are required to recall the response which had originally been learned to the compound. Thus the extent to which each component is effective in eliciting the response is an indication of whether it has been selected or extracted from the compound during learning. Those components which are most effective are therefore termed the selected stimuli. This method was pioneered by Underwood (1963). Stimulus selection is clearly a form of coding, in that the functional stimulus is in a different (because reduced) form from the nominal stimulus.

However, one difficulty is that the response in the test trial to the component might be mediated through the compound. In other words, the component (e.g. R) might be acting as a cue for the subject to reconstruct RXG. RXG would then be acting as the functional stimulus leading to the recall of the response term. Relations between components may have been learned, and as a result, this sort of mediation could occur. However, it does not necessarily follow that it does. In other words, the component could still be the functional stimulus for the response.

Results using this experimental technique have indicated that a subject selects components for many different reasons. He may choose a component which the experimenter suggests, which is signalled by some cue such as colour, or which has been used in prior learning. He may also choose those components that are more easily paired with the response term than are other components. He may, for example, choose a component that begins with the same letter as the response term. Or he may choose those components that are paired consistently in the experiment with a response term in preference to others which are not. It has also been found that once subjects start reliably selecting a component, learning is as efficient as when the component is itself presented as the nominal stimulus. But when the subject overlearns, other components besides the selected one start to be effective.

As Richardson (1972) concludes, 'all the evidence indicates that stimulus selection is the result of a learning strategy that is under the control of the subject. It is assumed to be the result of an active, organized, attentional process.' It may be conceived as a conscious reduction of the load placed on the coding system by an unfamiliar and hard-to-code item. Stimulus selection may be an early coding operation upon the nominal stimulus; other transformations may occur. For example, a component may be selected as the functional stimulus, and then be transformed into a familiar image or word in order to aid subsequent retrieval.

3.4.2 Hierarchical coding

Stimulus selection involves the selection of one part of the nominal stimulus for coding purposes. Hierarchical encoding refers to the use of one code to represent several nominal stimuli. The classic experiment demonstrating the usefulness of such a coding strategy is that of Miller (1956). He taught subjects to code sequences of binary digits, e.g. 010010110110, into decimal digits. 00 is coded as 0, 01 as 1, 10 as 2, and 11 as 3. The above sequence would thus be coded as 102312. These decimal digits could then be coded again into letters, thus 00 would be coded as A, 01 as B, 02 as C, 03 as D, 10 as E, etc. 102312 would be coded as ELG. Thus the final coding of the original sequence contains 25 per cent of the numbers of symbols presented. Subjects could recall twenty digits using this coding strategy, although they were limited to seven, plus or minus two, when they did not use it.

The implication of this approach is that the major function of coding is to provide an economical recoding device. It is not the multiplicity of attributes that is stressed, but the stage of recoding whereby from a brief code can be reconstructed a lengthy sequence. The decrease in the number of items to be retained has to be weighed against the number and complexity of the transformations required for reconstruction. The principle proponent of this view is N. F. Johnson (1970, 1972). He supposes that the coding contains all of the information about the nominal stimulus items that are required for serial recall: their identity, and their order. He sees codings as 'opaque'. That is, they do not *contain* this information, but only *represent* it. Therefore the subject may retain the coding, but he has still to retrieve the items. He has to decode the coding before he can recall them.

Johnson has employed a paired-associate procedure to support these hypotheses. His stimulus terms are the digits 1 and 2, and his response terms are series of letters. The first use of the technique to be discussed will be its employment to support the idea that the codings represent rather than contain the nominal stimulus items. If this is true, then a coding should be unique to its set of items. Even though a sequence contained many of the same letters as another, its coding should be different. Therefore the learning of a similar but not identical second pair of letter sequences should interfere with the recall of a first pair. Thus subjects learned, for example, the nine-letter, three-chunk sequence SBJ FQL ZNG as a response. They then learned slightly different sequences to the same stimuli, e.g. SXJ FQL TNG. The hypothesis that the coding of the second sequence would partially overlap with that of the first, and therefore cause retroactive interference when the first was subsequently recalled, was supported. When a letter in a chunk has been changed in the second sequence, there is only 50 per cent correct recall of the two unchanged letters in a chunk. Thus S and J in the example above would only be recalled successfully by 50 per cent of subjects. The changed letter, B, would only be recalled 40 per cent of the time. But a control group who did not learn the second sequence had a 90 per cent correct success rate. When four-letter chunks were used, it made no difference to the degree of interference whether one, two, or three letters were altered in the second sequence.

The same retroactive interference was found even when the same overall sequences were presented in the second learning session but chunked in a different way. Thus if SB JFQ LZ was one of the two sequences presented in the first list learned, then the learning of SBJ FQLZ would interfere with its retention in comparison with a control group who did no second-list learning. Further, the learning of SBJ FQLZ resulted in no superiority over a group who learned entirely different letters on the second list.

Thus it seems clear that individual codings represent particular chunks of items. This is also implied by the finding that transitional error probabilities are highest at chunk boundaries. Thus, given the sequence SBJ FQLZ, a subject is more likely to make an error on F given that he got J right than he is on Q given that he got F right. Moreover, it seems that subjects make all the decoding decisions about a chunk before they actually start recalling it out loud. In other words, there is a decode plus read-out two-process form of recall. This is suggested by experiments in which the length of chunks is varied. The longer the chunk, the more likely it is that the subject will have difficulty in decoding it, other things being equal. If he cannot decode all the items in a chunk, then he will not commence read-out at all. Therefore subjects are more likely completely to omit longer chunks than they are shorter ones. This finding is reported by Johnson (1972).

A final issue concerns the assertion that the coding contains the order as well as the item information contained in a letter sequence. It is maintained, in other words, that the items do not cue each other; rather, the coding contains all the order information required. When an item in a chunk was changed on a second presentation, the position in the chunk of the changed item made no difference to the degree of retroactive interference caused (see 2.5.2). Suppose, for example, that the middle item of a three-item chunk was changed. If recall of this item were a cue to the next, then the recall of the last item should be worse than that of the first. For the middle item would cue the former but not the latter. Thus there is no evidence that a sequential cueing process is operating. On the contrary, Johnson (1972) puts forward recent evidence that subjects can learn sequences by assigning single organizational positions to each item.

It must be stressed that all these results were obtained using material which is amenable only to certain restricted forms of coding. Letters of the alphabet cannot be expected to elicit much coding by semantic attributes, for example. Therefore the use of few attributes to create codings which could be recoded easily is rendered more likely. There is, furthermore, no great need to code by multiple attributes when the number of alternatives from which the correct item has to be retrieved is limited to the twenty-six letters of the alphabet. Not only, therefore, is the task and material likely to result in a reductive form of coding. Also, the experimenter cues the form of coding employed by presenting the sequences in chunks of letters. It has already been stressed that if subjects use cues provided by the experimenter, the inference to be drawn is that they *can* employ this form of coding, rather than that they habitually do so. Thus the reductive coding described in 3.4 may be typical of memory performance only in certain highly artificial tasks.

3.5 Summary

Chapters 2 and 3 have reviewed many different forms of coding. The techniques employed to show the considerable capacity of the sensory registration systems were first described. It was suggested that sensory registration performs the function of retaining presented information for long enough for coding and selection of the material to be stored to occur.

Next the coding of individual letters of the alphabet was discussed in the context of a series of experiments by Posner. By the use of a visual matching task, Posner was able to show that the letters were coded visually at different levels of abstraction as well as verbally. Next, the nature of verbal coding of letters by their names was considered more fully. It was shown that whether the codings were acoustic or articulatory in nature, they could only be accounted for in terms of the distinctive features of sounds. In other words, the coding was by means of a combination of several attributes.

The superiority of recall of material presented auditorily was then described; one possible explanation considered was that auditory presentation requires less transformations than visual if the material is coded verbally — a useful attribute when presentation is rapid. Other aspects of the presentation episode were considered as potential attributes by which material could be coded. The order of items in a list and the frequency of items within the list were two such aspects.

Various features of the material itself were also shown to be of potential value as coding attributes. It was shown that words could be coded by their denotative and connotative features. Release from proactive inhibition and incidental learning were cited as fruitful techniques in the investigation of these features. It was also demonstrated that subjects could and often did use various mediating devices when asked to learn a connection between two apparently unrelated items. However, it was stressed that the structure of verbal material is its most important characteristic. Any item longer than a word is coded in terms of its structure, since the subject's knowledge of the structural rules of his language is automatically applied to such material. It was suggested that the major structural variable is the complexity of the deep or underlying meaning of the material. The considerable evidence for coding in terms of visual imagery was reviewed, but it was not considered a mutually exclusive alternative to other forms of coding. Rather, it was taken to be one particular way in which coded attributes might be represented in memory.

Chapter 3 concluded with an account of two forms of coding which were primarily reductive in nature. Stimulus selection indicates that part only of the nominal stimulus may be coded, while hierarchical coding shows that it is possible to code a series of items into chunks in such a way that the coding of the chunk is an economic device for recoding. It was stressed, however, that most of the forms of coding described in the two chapters were elaborative rather than reductive in function.

However, certain obvious questions arise from the evidence reviewed in these chapters. Why are some forms of coding employed rather than others? How many of these forms of coding are employed on any one occasion? To what extent do codings remain invariant over the presentation-test interval? Can a distinction be made between conscious and unconscious levels of coding, or between different levels of coding? These questions have arisen incidentally in Chapters 2 and 3 (e.g. 2.2.5, 3.1.2). They will be considered in detail in Chapter 4.

Conditions of coding

4.1 Conscious and Automatic Coding

4.1.1 Multiplicity of Coding

In previous chapters the notion of coding by attributes has been used as a convenient explanatory device. In order for this device to have real explanatory power, however, lawful experimental relationships have to be established between other variables and the number, identity and function of the attributes coded. One immediate question concerns the *number* of attributes which the subject can employ. How many are required to uniquely specify an item or a set of items for retrieval purposes? And how many can the limited-capacity information processing system deal with?

Several types of evidence have already been cited which suggest that coding by several attributes of a single item may occur. Posner's work, for example (2.2.5), showed that a letter name could be coded in terms of its visual shape and its name, and that these attributes could coexist. Wickens (see 3.1.2) manipulated the number of attributes by which the final trial material differed from earlier material. He found that release from PI was greater when it differed along two attributes of affective meaning than when it differed along one. Also, the more unlike the original material the release material was in terms of its denotative meaning, the greater the release. Both these findings imply that the original material was encoded in terms of more than one attribute.

A second type of evidence which suggests that a large number of attributes are encoded is the incidental learning paradigm. Jenkins (see 3.1.3) has shown that a wide variety of attributes are encoded even when subjects are not aware that they are going to have to recall. Hintzman's work (2.5.2.) shows that, given an item that had been presented, subjects could retrieve all sorts of information about the conditions of its presentation.

Finally, the view of organizational coding proposed in the next chapter asserts that lists of unrelated items are coded by multiple attributes before any economies in coding can occur. For it is only after items have been coded that overlappings in item attributes can be coded and some economy effected. The immediate perception and use of a single or a very few attributes to code relations is, it will be suggested, only evidenced when the material is preselected to accord with a highly organized structure.

Perhaps, however, we are 'overloading memory' (Underwood, 1972); that is, perhaps we are assuming that more attributes are coded than is in fact the case in each particular event. The first source of evidence that this may be so concerns experimental technique. It relates to the possibility that subjects are primed by the experimental task to encode material according to the attributes which the experimenter expects to find. For example, in the release from PI paradigm the first three trials will consist of material related in a certain way, e.g. three sets of three animal words. The subject may be primed by their recurrence to code the words by their animal attribute(s), since this is the most perceptible feature of the material. To this extent, the paradigm suffers from the same shortcomings as the presentation of categorically related items in blocked form (5.2.3). In the incidental paradigm, on the other hand, there is the likelihood that the orienting instructions will result in the subject paying particular attention to a feature of presentation to which he would not otherwise have attended. The real interest of the incidental learning paradigm is not, then, in showing *how many* features are coded at any one time. Rather, it lies in comparisons between different orienting instructions in an effort to discover *which* features are more effective for coding (Craik and Lockhart, 1972).

4.1.2 The conscious-automatic distinction

However, these are technical objections. There are more for-
midable theoretical difficulties with the adoption of the
position that the number of coding attributes involved in the
coding of any particular event is immense. These difficulties
concern the limited capacity of the information processing
system. It will be argued in Chapter 7, with Broadbent (1971),
that there is a limit to the amount of information to which, at
any point in time, attention can be paid.

Clearly it will be impossible for attention to be focused on all
the attributes by which an item or items may be encoded.
Therefore, granted that these attributes are numerous, the
necessary conclusion is that they are not all consciously attended
to. Posner and Warren (1972) also distinguish between conscious
and unconscious automatic coding; and Atkinson and Juola
(1973) have employed the distinction specifically in their
theory of recognition. Posner and Warren suggest that when
items are coded by attributes, a direct connection is established
between presented material and well-learned codes in semantic
memory. That is, conscious attention is not required on the part
of the subject. If, then, one considers the forms of coding
specified in Chapters 2 and 3, it becomes evident that some
might tap semantic memory codes directly. Examples are the
name code for a letter, the phonological code for a word, the
grammatical code for a phrase, the affective code for a word.
Consider, however, other forms of coding described in those
chapters. The use of imagery, of natural language mediators, of
stimulus selection, and of rewriting into a shorter form, all imply
conscious attention. They all involve the conversion or transformation of the nominal stimulus into a different form, and its
subsequent retransformation by means of some tag giving the
rule for transformation. This appears at first sight to be wasteful,
since it requires the subject (a) to pay attention to a coded form
of the subject. If, then, one considers the forms of coding
transformed code plus an instruction tag. However, the reason
for this sort of coding has already been suggested. It is that it
permits the subject to employ existing semantic memory codes.

Thus in some situations it is proposed that direct access to
codes in semantic memory is available; in others, it is considered
that conscious attention has to be given to transforming the
material into such a form that it can tap these codes. Why should

this difference occur? The most likely answer appears to be in terms of the nature of the task. The more 'natural' and the more 'immediate' an experimental task is, the more likely the subject is to have direct access to the codes which have been acquired to deal with such situations. Thus the subject's reaction to an utterance consisting of a sentence is to code it automatically into its meaning code, since his linguistic skills have been developed specifically for the purpose of decoding utterances. Similarly, his reaction to being presented with a visual letter is to code it automatically into its sound, since this is the natural function of his knowledge of the written alphabet. However, his reaction when being presented with an explicitly memorizing task may be far more consciously controlled. He may devise mnemonics to decode and recode the material. The mnemonic code itself may be something he has learned well already (e.g. the 'one is a bun' technique, see 3.3.2). Or, in another situation in which unconnected items are being presented at a fast rate, he may select a strategy of keeping his attention on as many of the items as he can while they are being presented, using, perhaps, the acoustic-articulatory code of the word in order to do so. Or, finally, even in the typical categorical list, multi-trial free-recall task (see 5.1.1), he may consciously adopt a strategy of superordinate coding. Staff and Eagle (1971) have shown reports of awareness of use of this strategy to covary with degree of clustering.

Thus, the coding of items by attributes alone, derived directly from well-learned codes, may be considered to be at the automatic level; the coding by means of various transformations in order to be able to tap well-learned codes for their attributes may be considered to be at the conscious level. Since *both* types of coding employ the same codes, they may be expected to use the same attributes. Thus, for example, the subject may automatically encode the word 'lion' presented in a sentence in terms of its wild animal attribute(s). Given the same word in a group of four words blocked into a category, with the advance knowledge that he will have to recall the items, he may consciously attend to the items and perceive their category membership, tap his semantic structure, and apply the superordinate coding to the unit of four. In both cases he will have used the same attributes.

4.1.3 Evidence for the distinction

The inference from this approach is that one has to distinguish well-learned codes in semantic memory and strategies for using them. These will be discussed in Chapter 6. A prior task is to discuss the evidence on which the distinction between conscious and automatic (unconscious) coding is based. The distinction implies, firstly, a difference in the amount of time required to code; automatic coding should be faster. Secondly, it implies that tasks which do not require or permit attention should result in automatic coding. Thirdly, it predicts that responses to such tasks should reflect codes in a very direct way. Finally, it suggests that conscious coding should permit the subject to select one of several different forms of coding rather than being locked automatically into one; such selection would be in accord with task requirements, so that a *level* of coding to suit such features as type of material and time constraints could be selected.

Dealing first with the times required to code consciously and automatically, the speed of automatic coding has been noted. Posner's name code took slightly longer than his visual code, but both were performed in well under half a second. Wickens (see 3.1.2) has produced evidence that affective features may be coded even before a word's name is available to the subject. By way of contrast, conscious selection and application of a code may take considerable time; such forms of coding as natural language mediators and imagery are shown to increase over trials. Moreover, in those short-term memory tasks in which subjects rehearse, their rehearsal rapidly becomes incapable of dealing with incoming material if the input rate exceeds a certain speed (see Chapter 7). Conscious attention requires time.

The second and third implications of the conscious-automatic distinction outlined above were these: that tasks which do not require or permit attention should result in automatic coding, and that the existence of automatic coding is to be inferred from the extent to which the subject's coding directly taps the well-learned code. Thus a research strategy designed to test these implications would vary degree of attention required by the task as the independent and directness of the tapping of the code as the dependent variable. Unfortunately, we know too little about the codes in semantic memory (see Chapter 6) to be able to say what is and what is not a direct representation of them. However, there is one technique which has been used in the study of attention where a comparison between attended and unattended material can be made. This book has not dealt with attention theory (see Treisman, 1969), partly because a forthcoming volume in the present series will be concerned with attention and information processing. The technique employed by workers in this field which has particular relevance here is the dichotic listening task, by which one message is played into one ear, and a different one into the other. In some cases, the subject is instructed to listen to one ear only. Thus the other ear, or channel, is unattended. Characteristics of the message passed into the unattended ear are nevertheless coded. They include the sex of voice of the speaker, whether he is speaking in the same or a different language from the material on the attended channel, and even some content features. For example, transitional probabilities, i.e. the likelihood of one word following the previous one, can also be processed. The less physical or phonological differences there were between the two messages, the more likely the listener was to code the unattended message in terms of its meaning attributes. This evidence seems to suggest, then, that automatic coding taps the same codes as does conscious coding.

The problem of the directness of the tapping of structure remains to be solved. But there are some indications that the relationship between automatic and conscious coding is similar to that between sensory registration and automatic coding (see 2.1.3). That is, the function of automatic coding may be to retain a set of *attributes* in a fairly unorganized condition for the subject; he may then exercise his conscious attention upon them and organize them further. This leads to the counter-intuitive prediction that in some cases immediate recall should be inferior to delayed recall, a prediction which is borne out in chess player's memory for a position on the board (De Groot, 1965) and musician's memory for a sheet of music (Reicher and Haller, 1971, cited by Posner and Warren, 1972). Moreover, our comprehension of language indicates that we pay little attention to phonological and grammatical attributes of utterances, being *aware* of their semantic interpretation (Johnson—Laird, 1974).

If the strategy of varying the degree of attention required in the task and observing differences of coding 'directness' is not viable, the fourth implication of the automatic-conscious distinction has greater possibilities. It is that conscious coding permits the selection from alternative forms of coding. The appropriate research strategy is therefore to manipulate such features of a particular task as make the selection of some rather than other possible forms of coding more likely. The subject would be predicted to select a level of coding appropriate to the task requirements, and also be able to report awareness that he had done so (Wickens, 1970).

4.2 Levels of coding

4.2.1 Time constraints

The notion of levels of coding has recently been developed (Craik and Lockhart, 1972; Cermak, 1972) as an alternative to explicit information processing models which distinguish different stores within the system. The levels concept has been introduced in 1.3.4, and the distinction was employed in the titles of Chapters 2 and 3.

The evidence for the distinction between short-term and long-term stores is reviewed in 7.2.1, and the way in which the concept of levels of coding can provide an alternative framework is described in 7.4.1. Here we will consider the notion of levels of coding in the context of the conditions of coding: the independent variables which have an effect upon coding.

Craik and Lockhart (1972) suggest that just as there are levels of perceptual processing which start at the physical level of analysis but move on to the symbolic, given time, so coding processes in memory tasks may follow the same sequence (Massaro, 1970b). In the case of verbal material, the progression would be from less deep acoustic-articulatory features to deeper semantic features. Further, the deeper the level of coding, the better recall and recognition performance results. Thus Craik and Lockhart propose certain constraints upon coding. They suggest that forms of coding follow a certain sequence, and that it is the depth of coding reached that determines memory performance; and they maintain that greater conscious attention is required for deeper coding to occur.

One factor which would clearly be expected to affect the level of coding employed is that of time available for the task. Consider, for example, the typical free-recall task in which verbal items are presented at a fairly fast rate, often greater than one per second. The subject may only have time to code each item by its acoustic-articulatory features before the next item is presented. Shulman (1970) has shown that decreasing the rate of presentation from one item per 350 milliseconds through 700 to 1400 results in better performance with a semantic task. The task was to recognize a subsequent probe word as meaning the same as a presented item. The implication is, of course, that semantic coding in terms of the denotative attributes of a word takes some time. On the other hand, perhaps semantic coding in terms of connotative, affective meaning takes less time (see 3.1.2). Anyway, it seems likely that subjects adopt a strategy to enable them to pay more attention to such rapidly presented material and code it more deeply (see 7.3.2).

The finding of the 'negative recency' effect (Craik, 1970) lends support to this view. Normally, the last few items in a free-recall list are better recalled than the other items (the recency effect). However, this result only obtains when recall is required directly or very soon after presentation. When there is a considerable period between such an immediate recall trial and a delayed recall trial, the last few items are the *worst* recalled in the delayed trial. Craik suggests that this is because the last few items are only coded to an acoustic-articulatory level; this enables them to be recalled immediately (see 7.4.1), but results in poor subsequent retrieval. Craik (1973) showed that this result had to be attributed to the different level of coding which these latter items received. It could not be explained by the fact that they had spent less time being recirculated (see 7.3.1) by means of their acoustic-articulatory coding. He forced subjects to rehearse aloud the last items as often as the early ones, but still found that they were worse recalled after a delay. Indeed, such forced rehearsal may actively prevent earlier items from being properly encoded, since it has a depressing effect on their recall (Jacoby, 1973). Thus we may conclude that time constraints have their depressing effect because they prevent adequate encoding.

4.2.2 Degree and direction of attention
Another variable which should affect the depth of coding is the degree of attention which the subject can pay to the task. If a concurrent task is added which also requires attention, subjects would be expected to code less deeply. This was discovered by Eagle and Ortof (1967). Subjects had to code digits as well as listen to the words to be recalled; as a result, they

made more false recognitions in the subsequent recognition tests, which were based on acoustic-articulatory similarities. Other studies (Murdock, 1965; Silverstein and Glanzer, 1971) have shown similar effects of concurrent tasks on recall. While recall of most list items suffers as a result, that of the last few items does not. If the last few items are only encoded to an acoustic-articulatory level, however, this is explicable. The less deep level of coding may be automatic and require little attention; its function is to code the items in such a form as to hold them in circulation until deeper coding can be applied (see 7.3.1). Thus the last few items will be recalled as effectively when there is an additional interpolated task as when there is not.

Thus the *degree* of attention paid to the task will be a determinant of the level of coding employed. The *direction* of attention may also be a relevant factor. If the material is so presented that one particular attribute will be attended to, then that attribute will be used for coding purposes. Bruce and Crowley (1970) (2.3.3) only found long-term coding by acoustic-articulatory features when they presented the acoustically similar words in a group. The experimenter may also direct subjects' attention to a particular attribute by requiring a particular performance. Posner (1969), for example (2.2.1), required subjects to match a test item on the basis of its physical, letter-class, or acoustic similarity to the presented item. It is worth noting, however, that subjects were not inhibited entirely from coding by other attributes even when one attribute was specifically selected for them in this way. The subject's expectations of the task will also affect the attributes attended to. Frost (1971) found that when subjects thought they were going to have to recognize pictures, they coded them by particular visual characteristics; if they thought they were going to have to recall, they were more likely to code verbally.

The most clear-cut evidence for the effect of directing the subjects' attention, however, is the incidental learning paradigm employed by Jenkins and his colleagues (see 3.1.3). Subjects are oriented towards particular attributes of material at presentation without, nevertheless, being aware that they will be required to recall. Results show that recall performance is dependent upon the attribute to which attention has been paid.

4.2.3 Depth of coding and performance — the evidence

Craik and Lockhart (1972) maintained also that the deeper the coding, the better the memory performance. There seems to be overwhelming evidence that both recall and recognition performance is better when coding is semantic than when it is acoustic-articulatory. The ̆ incidental learning paradigm, for example, results in better recall when subjects have previously been oriented to semantic rather than grammatical attributes. In a recent experiment, Elias and Perfetti (1973) found that recognition varies as a function of the level of coding which the subject was instructed to use. Subjects instructed to code words into synonyms did better than those instructed to code by an associate. Both groups did better than a group merely told to learn, while a group instructed to code by acoustic-articulatory attributes performed worst of all. Wood (1972) found that prior semantic sorting or classifying resulted in better free recall than prior acoustic-articulatory sorting and classifying. Finally, Gardiner (1974) found an important interaction — the superiority of semantic coding is greater when more than one attribute is coded (although acoustic-articulatory coding resulted in poor recall regardless of the number of attributes).

One point worth making in passing is that both recall *and* recognition performance improve as a function of level of coding. Traditional views of recognition (Kintsch, 1970a) suggest that recognition and recall differ in that recognition requires only a decision as to whether the test item did in fact occur at presentation. Recall requires retrieval. Expressed in terms of coding theory, the traditional theory assumed that the recognition task only made use of the occurrence attribute, whether or not the item had occurred at presentation. Recent work reviewed by Mandler (1972) indicates that this is not so. He found that subjects *did* use other attributes within the recognition task. He used his technique of subjects first sorting 'unrelated' items to a criterion, then trying to recognize subsequently presented test items as the same or different (old or new). He discovered that the more groupings a subject had used, the more likely he was to recognize the items correctly. Similarly, the verbal context of an item affects the extent to which it is recognized; when a noun with alternative meanings is presented with an adjective which makes its meaning clear, it is worse recognized subsequently when the context is different than when the original context is retained (Light and Carter-Sobell, 1970); and when a word is presented paired with an associate, it is better recognized at test provided the context is the same (Tulving and Thomson, 1971).

Mandler's work goes further, however. He goes on to show which sorts of information are coded by the occurrence attribute, and which by organizational, semantic attributes. By presenting two lists, he was able to demonstrate that subjects used occurrence coding to state which list an item was from. However, the decision as to whether an item was from one of the lists or whether it was a new item was more effectively made when the lists were more organized. So was the decision whether a synonym of the presented word was in fact presented. Thus codings of different sorts facilitate different aspects of performance. The notion of levels of codings is as appropriate in the analysis of recognition as it is in that of recall. Indeed, Mandler obtained a result very reminiscent of the negative recency effect in free recall. He found that the correlation between degree of semantic organizational coding and recognition performance was higher after two weeks' delay than with an immediate recognition test. This implies that occurrence coding is lost sooner than semantic coding. The longer the presentation-recognition interval, the more likely the subject is to try to retrieve the test item by means of its organizational coding as a check to see whether it did or did not occur. As a result, he often falsely recognizes as having been presented items which were in fact categorically related intrusions in an earlier attempt at recall. That is, he retrieves again for recognition purposes an item which he had falsely retrieved before, at recall.

4.2.4 Depth of coding and performance — the explanation
Given, then, that greater depth of coding results in improved recall and recognition performance, how can this be explained? One obvious answer is to suggest that semantic coding results in a greater number of attributes being encoded. Therefore retrieval should be more effective, since more attributes means better discrimination of the to-be-retrieved item from other items in semantic memory. This increased effectiveness should be evidenced in both recall and recognition performance if recognition, too, requires retrieval. One obvious test of this hypothesis would be that recall cues should only be effective if they reinstate the

same *level* of coding as the subject had reached at presentation. Further evidence is presented in the next section. However, it is worth noting that cues are particularly effective if they are at the same level as coding which had occurred. Consider (for example) the evidence concerning prompted recall of sentences. When sentences are coded in terms of the surface structure as indexed by pauses, then the position of the prompt word (recall cue) in relation to these pauses determines the response latency (Wilkes and Kennedy, 1969). However, when the meaning of the sentence is coded, a pronoun which refers to the subject of the sentence is the most effective prompt (Lesgold, 1972). Similarly, if the meaning of a sentence is changed on the fourth trial, release from PI occurs, but not if the grammatical form is changed (Schubert, Lively and Reutener, 1973).

There are, however, additional possible reasons why performance should be improved as a result of depth of coding. One is that the deeper the coding, the more time has been spent in coding the item. Another is that the deeper the coding, the more different forms of coding are available. The point is not that more *attributes* are available (which is why semantic coding is so effective). It is rather that a progression from less deep through to deeper levels of coding will result in more *forms* of coding being available for reconstruction purposes. Thus when semantic coding fails by itself as a means of reconstruction, acoustic-articulatory features, for example, can be brought to bear on the problem.

Just such a situation is found in the tip-of-the-tongue phenomenon (Brown and McNeill, 1966). They read dictionary definitions of words to subjects, thus providing them with semantic attributes. There were some occasions when subjects could not construct the appropriate word, but felt it was on the tip-of-the-tongue. Sometimes they could produce the initial sound of the word, or its length in terms of number of syllables. In other words, they were employing acoustic-articulatory coding to assist semantic coding. Admittedly, the experiment was tapping semantic memory — it was not an episodic task. And the experimenter engineered the sequence semantic—acoustic. A related result was found by Gardiner, Craik and Bleasdale (1973). They asked subjects to produce words in response to dictionary definitions of those words. They found that the longer the subject took to produce a word, the more likely that word was to be subsequently recalled, provided that the subject felt that he knew it. This implies that the number of attributes required before the word could be produced affected the ease with which it was recalled. It does not seem justifiable to suggest, with Craik and Lockhart (1972, p. 682), that 'since the organism is normally concerned only with the extraction of meaning from the stimuli, it is advantageous to store the products of such deep analyses, but there is normally no need to store the products of preliminary analyses'. This seems absolutely true of the normal task of the *listener* in the communication setting; however, in an episodic memory task, the subject also has to reconstruct the stimulus verbatim. His behaviour may be analogous to that of the *speaker* in the communication situation, who, of course, has to code phonologically and grammatically as well as meaningfully (see 7.5.1). At any rate, it seems fair to leave open the possibility that the number of different forms of coding as well as the particular form reached may be determinants of effectiveness of performance.

Other questions about the levels of coding concept will be raised in 7.4.2. Here it is worth questioning whether the order of coding is always from form to meaning. Do the formal, less deep, stages *have* to be passed through before semantic coding can occur? Second, the treatment of the semantic level requires refinement; one must surely hypothesize different levels of semantic coding. The experiment of Elias and Perfetti, quoted above, found that coding a word in terms of its synonym resulted in better recognition than coding in terms of an associate. Experiments on the perception and comprehension of language (6.2.1, 6.2.2) support this approach also.

The concepts of automatic and conscious coding and of levels of coding should be considered together. It is quite possible that the emphasis laid by Craik and Lockhart on the attention required for conscious coding to a deep level is misplaced. A situation in which a conscious effort is required to code semantically may be the exception rather than the rule. The fact that semantic coding takes longer does not necessarily imply that it has to be conscious.

As was suggested above, the automatic coding may normally be adequate. When more contrived, conscious elaborative coding is required, then the automatic coding may have already provided the basic attributes upon which such further elaboration could be based. Nevertheless, the concept of levels of coding seems to be a welcome advance from information processing flow diagrams, and provides a conceptual basis on which subsequent research and theory should be built.

4.3 Coding specificity and variability

4.3.1 The encoding specificity hypothesis

The view of levels of coding implies that forms of coding are employed which are appropriate to the task. In recognition and recall tasks, therefore, the inference is that subjects will employ for recognition or retrieval purposes those codings which they applied at presentation. The encoding specificity principle 'emphasizes the importance of encoding events at the time of input as the primary determinant of the storage format and retrievability of information in the episodic memory system' (Tulving, 1972, p. 392). Specifically, it states, 'no cue . . . can be effective unless the to-be-remembered item is specifically encoded with respect to that cue at the time of storage' (Thomson and Tulving, 1970, p. 255). It should be noted that the encoding specificity hypothesis does *not* state that all the encodings of an item must be reinstated at recall for the item to be recognized or retrieved. Such a position would be contrary to the notion of levels of coding, which supposes that some attributes may be coded but not retained for retrieval purposes. It must also be noted that the encoding specificity hypothesis, if correct, renders untenable theories of free recall which suggest that items are coded and stored individually and general language habits are used at recall to generate appropriate items (Slamecka, 1968). For it stresses the importance of coding on a particular occasion, i.e. as a feature of episodic memory.

The experiments carried out to test the hypothesis have mostly varied the context of the to-be-recalled item at presentation and test, or kept it constant (Tulving and Osler, 1968; Thomson and Tulving, 1970). The items have been presented paired with an associate (as defined by the free association norms). Then either the same or a different (but equally frequent) associate is provided at recall as a cue. Results show that recall and recognition improve as a result of the recall cue being the same as the presentation cue even when they are only weak associates. On the other hand, even when the recall cue is a strong associate of the item, whereas the presentation cue was a (different) weak one, recall is not improved over a no-cue control condition.

The inference that recall cues must reinstate codings at input is not contradicted by findings (Bahrick, 1969) that strong associates presented at recall only are effective. For it could reasonably be supposed that the items were coded by the subject himself at input in terms of these strong associates. The same result was not obtained with weak associates.

A clever variant of this technique has been employed by Bobrow and Light (cited in Bower, 1970b). They used ambiguous words, coded by one meaning at presentation, and another at recall. So, for example, they used such adjective-noun pairs as 'chirping cardinal', or 'church cardinal'. The retrieval cue 'bird' was effective for cardinal in the former but not the latter case (subjects were American!).

These experiments focus on the coding of items rather than subjective units. However, the results of Tulving and Pearlstone (1966) and Dong and Kintsch (1968) suggest that the same principle applies in the latter case. These workers show that the codings provided as cues at presentation by the experimenter for categories (Tulving and Pearlstone) or by the subject for his own sortings (Dong and Kintsch) are effective at retrieval. It should be noted, however, that they do not explicitly test the encoding specificity principle, since they do not provide different cues at presentation and recall. Mandler and Pearlstone's (1966) finding that subjects were far slower to learn lists in units sorted by others than they were to learn units sorted by themselves adds further support to the encoding specificity hypothesis.

Several additional points must be made at this juncture. First, it does not follow that because associated words are effective cues at presentation and recall, therefore the subject codes items in terms of their associates. Even in these experiments themselves, the items may have been coded in terms of the semantic attributes they shared with their associates. The recall cue therefore serves to reinstate this coding, rather than act as a coding itself. An analogy is to be found in the false recognition paradigm (see 3.1.3), where associates of presented words are falsely recognized as having occurred at presentation. Here again, it need not be assumed that it is an associative coding of the item which has been mistaken for the item itself; rather the coding of the associate shares enough attributes with the coding of the item to be mistaken for it. Finally, the important finding of McLeod, Williams and Broadbent (1971), that the effect of two associates rather than one as recall cues is more than additive, indicates that the encoding specificity hypothesis cannot identify codings with cues.

4.3.2 Coding variability

If the distinction between the nominal and the functional stimulus is maintained, then it becomes evident that the same nominal item may be encoded in different ways on different occasions (see Martin, 1968, 1972). Clearly, the presentation situation and the test situation of a memory task are different occasions. The decoding situation will be different from the encoding situation in many ways, and therefore there may not be a complete reinstatement of the presentation codings at recall. This does not run counter to the encoding specificity hypothesis, since the hypothesis does not maintain that the retrieval cue must reinstate the presentation coding in its entirety.

Consider some of the features of memory paradigms. In the multi-trial free-recall task, for example, material is usually presented in a different random order of items on each trial. Therefore any one item will be presented in a different context of other items from one trial to the next. Blocked presentation of categorical material or same-order presentation of unrelated material over trials results in constant rather than variable coding, however. In the case of blocked presentation, this constancy is only in terms of having items from the same category presented in the context of the item; for in the blocked presentation technique, the order of items within categories and the order of categories within the list is varied over trials. In the case of same-order presentation of unrelated items, a particular item always occurs in the same position with regard to the same other items. The same applies to blocked presentation of categorical specific paradigm employed.

There are, however, other features of the experimental situation not peculiar to the particular paradigm employed (see 2.5.5). The experimenter's instructions, his appearance and manner, the time of day, the time of year (see Pollio, 1968) and the particular format in which material is presented (Strand, 1970) are typical features external to the subject. The subject's alertness, motivation, attitude towards the experimenter, current preoccupations and subconscious trains of thought are all internal features which may or may not covary with the external ones. Moreover, any subsequent experimental event must take into account any previous experimental event as part of its context, since it must be supposed that the previous result has affected the subject in some way (Voss, 1972).

These features are so many and varied that it would be impossible to control them in an experimental situation, even if this were desirable. Instead, it seems reasonable to conceptualize them as 'contextual drift' (Bower, 1972a), *and to consider this encoding variability as a potential condition of successful encoding.* The reasons for this last suggestion are much the same as those advanced to account for the development of subjective units in the multi-trial free recall of unrelated items (see 5.4.3). That is, it may be supposed that the more attributes by which an item is coded, the greater the probability that it will share some attributes with another item. Therefore, the greater the probability that a coding of a relation will be set up by which both items may be retrieved; also, the greater the probability that retrieval of one item will cue retrieval of the other. Even artificially considering an item as an individual event which is presented on several different occasions, then coding variability should aid recall. For the subject will have several sets of situational attributes by which to code the item; therefore, he will have more attributes by which the item may be uniquely defined, and his retrieval will be more successful. If this picture is accurate, then coding variability works hand in hand with coding specificity. For since it results in more attributes, it makes it more likely that some cue which occurs at recall will reinstate an attribute employed for encoding purposes.

4.3.3 Evidence for coding variability

To justify these suggestions, experimental evidence must be adduced. At first sight, the evidence argues against the proposition that encoding variability aids recall. Experiments will be quoted (see 5.2.3) which show that constant order of repeated input of unrelated items results in better recall than random items. The same applies to blocked presentation of categorical order. Category codings or serial learning are strategies which, if adopted, should result in highly effective storage and retrieval.

Blocked and constant-order presentation strongly suggest such strategies to the subject, whereas random-order presentation conceals them. The comparison in these experiments is not, therefore, between constant and variable coding, but between induced strategy and variable coding. Obviously, variable coding will come off worse in any such comparison. This error was avoided in an experiment by Bevan, Dukes and Avant (1966). They showed that memory for superordinate category labels increased as the number of different instances of the category provided by the experimenter increased, thus showing that coding variability can aid recall.

A completely different approach is described by Martin (1972) and Voss (1972). This employs the paired-associate tasks, and one variant defines the variability of a nonsense syllable operationally as the number of different words it elicits as the first free associate over 100 subjects (Butler and Merikle, 1970). In other words, an item is said to be highly variably encoded if there are a large number of different words it elicits. It was found that when the nonsense syllable was the stimulus term, in the paired-associate task and a digit the response term, then learning was better for the more variably encoded nonsense syllables. Thus, when an item has a cue function, encoding variability is beneficial.

Another type of experimental evidence relates to the Melton effect (Melton, 1970). If an item is repeated within a list, then it is retained better the greater the number of intervening items between first and second presentation. It might be supposed that the further away from each other the occurrences of the item are, the greater difference between the two contexts of the item, and therefore between their encodings. Melton reviews the evidence which suggests that the lag effect is a very orderly relation up to an asymptote of from twenty to forty intervening words between the two item presentations. One alternative explanation (Waugh, 1970) is that less attention (rehearsal) time is devoted to a closely subsequent repetition, since the subject is seeking to rehearse as many different items as possible to optimize his performance. He is more likely to recognize a closely subsequent repetition as a repetition (Melton, 1967) and therefore not worthy of attention. However, support for the encoding variability interpretation is provided by Madigan (1969). He provided cues with the two presentations of the item, and also sometimes at recall. These cues were either the same or different (e.g. speed≃ENGINE, speed≃ENGINE, versus speed≃ENGINE, value≃ENGINE). If the lag effect were due to encoding variability, then the explicit provision of such variability for all items regardless of degree of lag should eliminate the lag effect. This was found, but only when *recall* was cued. In other words, the importance of encoding variability is at the retrieval end of the task, where the increase in codings provided by variability is valuable in uniquely defining the item.

The tentative conclusion must be that there are indications that coding specificity and coding variability are two sides of the same coin. The former stresses the importance of reinstating at least one input coding at recall, the latter the importance of ensuring that there *are* such codings common to both situations.

4.4 Summary

It was argued that there was some limit to the number of attributes by which material could be coded. It was proposed that a distinction between automatic and conscious coding was justified. This distinction permits the limit to be localized in the conscious process, specifically, in terms of the number of attributes to which attention can be paid at any one time. It was argued that automatic coding tapped structures in semantic memory directly, thus permitting many attributes to be coded in a very short period. The scanty evidence for the distinction was reviewed, and the strongest emphasis was placed on the subject's selection of attributes to accord with task requirements.

It was supposed that subjects would code to different levels, depending on such features of the experiment as time constraints, perceptual salience of certain features, etc. It was proposed that better recall resulted from deeper level (e.g. semantic) coding partly because the less deep levels are also available for reconstruction.

The importance of the encoding specificity principle was emphasized. If a coding is to be used to retrieve or recognize an item subsequently, it must be reinstated at that time. Evidence showing that this is so was reviewed. It was also shown that on different occasions (e.g. on different presentation trials of a list, on different presentations of an item, or on test as opposed to training trials) different codings of the same nominal item will occur. This coding variability is a result of the different internal and external contexts of presentation. It was concluded that variability made it more likely that a coding would be reinstated at recall or recognition, since it increased the number of overall encoding attributes.

CHAPTER 5

Organizational coding

5.1 Introduction

5.1.1 Multiple items

The distinction between this chapter and Chapters 2 and 3 hinges again on the distinction between the nominal and the functional. In those chapters, consideration was given to the way in which individual items were coded. These items ranged from visually presented letters through words to sentences. They all had in common the fact that they were *items*: that is, they were the nominal rather than the functional unit. It was the experimenter, not the subject, who defined what an item was. Chapters 2 and 3 showed how individual items were transformed by means of sundry different attributes.

It is clear that such an approach can only partially describe how subjects code the presentation episode. For in a typical presentation phase of a memory experiment, *several* items are presented (see 1.4.1). There is no justification for the assumption that subjects code visual lists or auditory sequences of items item by item. In other words, experimenter-defined and subject-defined units may differ (Tulving, 1968).

Not only may there be differences between nominal and functional units in terms of their *size*. Also, the *order* of items as presented and as coded may differ (Rundus and Atkinson, 1970). For example, given a randomly ordered list of items, some of which are animals, the subject may rehearse the animals together during the presentation (Rundus, 1971). Moreover, the principles underlying the order of items in the subject's recall and the experimenter's analysis of that order may also differ. For example, Cofer and Bruce (1965) expected to find nouns clustered together in free recall, adjectives in another cluster, verbs in another, and so on. They failed to find any great degree of clustering, so concluded that grammatical parts of speech were not a potent organizational feature. However, Stanners (1969) looked for and found in plenty groupings such as adjective plus noun, which the generative nature of the linguistic system would predict (see 3.2.1). The grammatical groupings which the earlier experimenters looked for were not those which subjects themselves used.

Thus nominal and functional definitions of unit size and item order may differ. The obvious inference for experimental *practice* is to analyse results in terms of number of functional units recalled rather than in terms of number of nominal items; and of subject-defined rather than experimenter-defined order. The inference for coding *theory* is the need to extend the notion of coding by attributes beyond the item level. It will be proposed in this chapter that *lists* of items as well as individual items are coded in terms of their attributes.

It has already been shown (2.5.2) that such features as position of the item within the list and position of the item in relation to other specific items may be employed. However, it is also apparent (Voss, 1972) that other *relations between items* are coded. Suppose all the words in a list are coded into a large number of different attributes of the types described in the previous chapters. In the case of some words some of the coding attributes will be identical. The number of coding attributes shared in this way will of course vary. 'Cat' and 'dog' may share more attributes than 'cat' and 'greenfly'. 'Dog' and 'cat' may therefore be said to be more closely related for the subject than 'cat' and 'greenfly'. If one says the relation between 'dog' and 'cat' is coded, one implies that those attributes which the items have in common are coded as a unit. The remaining attributes which the items do not share will be coded separately, and will serve to distinguish the two items from each other and from other items for storage and retrieval purposes.

This proposal, it is argued, satisfies the findings that related items are recalled together and more effectively than unrelated items; and it explains how the right items are recalled. It allows, in other words, both for the reductive and for the elaborative functions of coding — the reduction of the load on the system and the need to identify carefully each item for retrieval purposes.

It will also be noted that this proposal permits a single item to be coded in more than one way. For an item X may have a relation with other items Y and Z and a different relation with items U, V and W. In other words, item X will share certain of its attributes with Y and Z, and certain others with U, V and W. Thus, the recall of item X is not dependent upon one relational coding alone. It should be stressed that the attributes concerned in these codings need not necessarily be semantic in nature. They could, for example, be derived specifically from the presentation episode, and refer to such features as the order of the item in the presentation sequence. The above theoretical outline is expanded in 5.4.3.

5.1.2 Two traditions

The two main approaches to the analysis of organization in recall have concentrated on one function of coding largely to the exclusion of the other. The reductive function has been emphasized in experiments in which material is selected and results analysed in terms of the superordinate—subordinate hierarchical relationship (see 2.4.2). That is, it has been assumed that several items are coded by means of a single superordinate coding. This involves a very considerable degree of constraint of the situation by the experimenter; for by selecting the items on a categorical basis (e.g. four animals, four items of clothing, four proper names, etc.) and by analysing the order of recall on the same basis, he effectively ignores all other possible methods of organization the subject may employ. If he is to generalize from this experimental situation, he must assume that organization is in neat and tidy units, with each item being coded only within one unit.

The second tradition in the study of organizational coding, stressing the elaborative function, is less constrained by the experimenter. It seeks to show how subjects code relations between nominally unrelated words. However, the explanations are couched in terms of associative networks of words. That is, it is assumed that the relation between two words presented in a list is coded by the number of word associates they have in common, while the number of word associates peculiar to each word in particular serves to individuate it. The distinction between this tradition and the proposal outlined above is that the elaborative tradition supposes that words are coded by means of other words, the present writer that they are coded by attributes.

In other words, it can be argued that both the main traditions have underestimated the difference between the nominal and the functional; the reductive tradition assumes the identity of the subject's coding and the experimenter's categories, while the associative tradition assumes that coding is in the same form as presentation, viz., verbal.

The uses of the term *organization* have differed in accordance with the traditions of research they exemplify. In the reductive tradition, Mandler (1967, p. 330) states 'a set of objects or events are said to be organized when a consistent relation among the members of the set can be specified, and, specifically, when membership of the objects or subsets (groups, concepts, categories, chunks) is stable and identifiable', This definition implies more that the relations exist in the material than that they are imposed by the subject. Further, it implies that the items are members of only one unit each. Tulving (1968, p. 16) specifies the subject's output as being the crucial evidence for organization which 'occurs when the output order of items is governed by semantic or phonetic relations among items or by the subject's prior extra-experimental or intra-experimental acquaintance with the items constituting a list'. While this definition does not imply orderly membership of items in a class, it does specify certain attributes as being the basis for organizational coding. As Postman (1972, p. 39) remarks, 'if it is the activity of imposing structure on the materials which is at the heart of the concept, then the specific bases on which items are grouped or a retrieval plan is formulated may not have to be included among the defining criteria of organization'.

Voss (1972, p. 176) offers the following: 'Organization is a process that intervenes between input and output in such a way that input is increased in its systematization, and in such a way that there is not a 1:1 input-output relation.' While Voss emphasizes the subject's imposition of system or structure, it is worth noting that this systematization does not necessarily imply, as he maintains, a difference between order of input and order of output. Take, for example, the situation in which items are presented blocked together in a perfectly categorized order. The subject may use the semantic features to code the items by categories, and he may as a result recall them in exactly the same order as they are presented. He has coded the items not individually but systematically. Once again, the distance between the nominal and the functional is underestimated. Just as a word is presented as a word and recalled as a word but stored as a set of attributes, so with a list of words. Difference between input and output order is a useful index of organization; it is not a necessary condition for it.

Perhaps one of Wood's (1972) definitions is general enough. He proposes that organizational processes 'can be viewed as grouping operations which result in the direct linking of the to-be-recalled events'. If this definition is amended to allow for the probability that it is codings of the items which are linked, not the items themselves; and if it permits the possibility of multiple linkings of any particular item coding, this definition seems the most acceptable.

The main bodies of research deriving from the reductive and the elaborative traditions will be described in turn. It will be shown that many of the problems they raise may be attributed to an underestimate of the difference between nominal and functional stimuli; and that they may best be solved by the extension of the attribute coding idea to the multi-item situation. A penetrating review of the whole field of organization is provided by Postman (1972) and a thorough one by Wood (1972).

5.2 The reductive tradition

5.2.1 The strong hypothesis
A repeated finding in the use of free-recall learning tasks has been that subjects employ the relations inherent in material to aid their recall. It has been found that, given random-order presentation, recall has been ordered in a principled (i.e. a non-random) way; that the degree of principled ordering is correlated with the amount recalled; and that the values of both these variables increase over trials. Closer analysis of the recall protocols has revealed that it is an increase in the number of items per subjective unit that results in the overall increase in items recalled; it is not an increase in the total number of subjective units.

Mandler (1967) devised a particular technique of free-recall learning to establish that the reductive function of organizational coding accounted for these results. His subjects each sorted a set of nominally unrelated words into as many subsets as they wished. Having ensured that all the subjects' sortings were reliable over several trials, he then unexpectedly required recall. He found that the amount recalled increased linearly as a function of number of sets into which the items had been sorted. This relation only held for up to seven sets, however. His own and other research has shown that the number of items per unit which can be recalled is likewise limited to around seven. On the other hand, the two variables, number of units and number of items per unit, vary independently of each other. It has been difficult to separate the two analytically in the design of experiments (Shuell, 1969). However, manipulations of independent variables have proved effective. For example, labels for units provided at recall by the experimenter result in an increase in the number of units recalled but not in the number of items per unit (Tulving and Pearlstone, 1966).

Mandler concluded from his results that the limitations of immediate memory span were applicable in the free-recall task. He supposed that there is a strict upper limit to the number of units which subjects can store. This limit he supposed to be that discovered by Miller (1956) of up to seven. The function of organization is therefore to chunk the presented material into any number of chunks up to this upper limit, since a chunk is taken to be a unit as far as processing capacity is concerned. As organization proceeds over trials in a multi-trial free-recall procedure, units become larger and better formed. Thus more items can be passed through the information processing system from short-term into long-term storage. This point of view is supported by the finding that although the number of unrelated items recalled is less than the number of categorically related items, the number of units is the same. In other words, categorizable items are easier to unitize, and so are better recalled.

However, there are certain objections to this 'strong' reductive hypothesis (Postman, 1972). First, some empirical evidence: it has been found that when the Mandler procedure was reversed in such a way that subjects' sorting criterion succeeded rather than preceded recall, no relation was found between number of units *sorted* and number of items recalled. A relation was found, however, between number of units *recalled* and number of items recalled. This suggests that the locus of the limitation may be at the retrieval rather than the storage phase. Thus Mandler's stress on the limits of *initial* information-processing capacity may be mistaken. This emphasis on the retrieval phase is elaborated in the next section (5.2.2). However, the strong reductive hypotheses, setting an upper limit on the number of units which can be recalled, runs into further difficulties. It has been shown that more units can be recalled when longer lists of items are presented, even though the size of the units remains constant. Moreover, it is conceivable that, given adequate practice, subjects could recall more than seven units in those task situations where this limit appears to operate. One may postulate superchunks. However, it seems less risky to abandon the notion of strict upper limits to processing capacity.

5.2.2 Organization at retrieval

An alternative approach has been to suggest that organization has in general a reductive function since there are limits on the information processing capacity. However, according to this view, the limits may not be so much on the number of units which can be passed through into storage. Rather, they might be more on the number of stored units which can be retrieved from storage at recall. At recall, many items may be available but not accessible. That is, many codings of subjective units may not be used by the subject at recall. If they were used, many more items could be retrieved and recalled. This was made clear in an experiment by Tulving and Pearlstone (1966). They presented subjects with categorized lists of words, together with category labels. For some subjects, they repeated the labels at recall, while for others they did not. Those subjects who were provided with retrieval cues in this way remembered more items than those who were not. However, this superiority was in terms of number of categories of items recalled only, not in terms of number of items per category. The conclusion was that although subjects had stored the items by means of category codings, they could not provide themselves with those codings at recall.

There is a considerable amount of other evidence which suggests that subjects employ codings of relations at retrieval. One particularly strong form of evidence indicates that when interference occurs, it is at the unit rather than at the item level. If subjects are given one list to remember followed by a second, interference may occur between the two. However, when the words in the lists are from semantic categories, retroactive interference is at the category, not the item level (Tulving and Psotka, 1971). In other words, less units are remembered, not less items per unit. Similarly, these effects of interference may be counteracted if the experimenter provides category cues at recall (Strand, 1971).

A second type of evidence (e.g. Pollio, Richards and Lucas, 1969) concerns the temporal characteristics of recall of categorizable material. Items within a category cluster are recalled in short bursts, with little time between items. However, there is a longer gap between the last item in one category and the first in another than between items within categories. This latter gap increases as the recall phase progresses from one category to another, implying that the later category codings are not so easily available to the subject.

Finally, there is the interesting 'some or none' effect (Cohen, 1966). That is, if a category of items is recalled at all, then several of its member items are recalled. Single items from a category are seldom remembered. Further, when category labels are actually included among the items to be recalled, they are recalled at the head of the list of their category members.

5.2.3 Coding and amount recalled

All these findings suggest that relational codings are employed for retrieval purposes. Some of them show that the use of codings results in a greater number of items being recalled. The relation of measures of clustering to amount recalled has also been investigated frequently. Measures of clustering are based on a comparison between the number of occasions when any two items from the same category occur adjacently in recall, and the number of occasions when this would be expected to occur by chance. The greater the difference, the higher the degree of clustering. In general, positive correlations between clustering and amount recalled have been found. However, these findings must be treated with caution (Colle, 1972). Firstly, the positive correlations may be artefacts of the measures of clustering; for in the case of some measures, the optimum possible level of clustering increases with number of items recalled. Second, correlations have often been evidenced over all subjects, but seldom within treatment groups; the increase in degree of correlation which one would predict as a result of, for example, the provision of cues at recall as compared with their absence has not been reported. Third, there is evidence which suggests that it is only very high levels of clustering which result in increased recall. Puff (1970a), for example, found that when he divided his subjects into groups, high and low clusterers, there was no difference in amount recalled between them. It has since been found that it is only when the subjects who cluster highest are compared with those who cluster lowest, with the middle range omitted, that differences in amount recalled are found (Thompson, Hamlin and Roenker, 1972).

It is possible that it is only when subjects adopt in its entirety the neatly ordered set of categorized chunks provided for them in the material by the experimenter that recall of categorizable material is improved. Support for this suggestion is provided by the findings that blocked presentation results in the most reliable increases in recall. That is, when the items are presented in categorical sequence recall is better than in the situation in which the subject has to perceive the categorical relations in a randomly ordered set of items. Similarly, simultaneous as opposed to successive presentation of items results in increased recall (Puff and Bousfield, 1967), since it permits the relations between items to be more easily perceived. The improvement resulting from the presentation of items in a multiple hierarchy, with units, subunits, sub-subunits and items is even greater (Bower, Clark, Lesgold and Winenz, 1969). In sum, modes of presentation which make it absolutely clear to the subject that chunks of items are neatly packaged in equal portions result in greater recall than when subjects have to discover the basis for organization themselves.

This is hardly surprising. What it shows is that subjects *can* use such obvious aids; it does not show that they habitually *do* use this form of structure when they actively code material which is not so neatly packaged. The high degree of clustering evidenced in subjects' recall shows only that subjects had no alternative but to follow the experimenter's organization. It is only when clustering is considerably less than maximal that the possibility arises that subjects were actively using other codings of relations not provided by the experimenter. Ironically, lower clustering may point to greater active organization!

There are, furthermore, many other features of material which subjects have been shown to use if they are provided. For example: words each beginning with a different letter of the alphabet; items of similar visual shape; words which rhyme; words of different logical relationships to each other (e.g. subordinate, coordinate, superordinate); synonyms; and words with similar imagery components. In all cases, subjects employed the relationship cited in order to group or order items and recall them better. Because the clustering measure is one of the only two measures of regularities in order of recall of items, it was used in most of the above cases. But it does not follow that the simple chunking organization which the clustering measure implies is the preferred mode of activity of the subject in any other than a few atypical situations.

Indeed, when the other measure of organization is applied to the subjects' recall of categorizable material, it becomes clear that the superordinate-subordinate relationship is not the only one employed by the subject even here. The second sort of measure is termed the inter-trial repetition measure (ITR) (Bousfield and Bousfield, 1966). It is simply an indication of consistencies of order between items over two recall trials. Thus if an item, a, is followed immediately by another, b, on both trial 1 and trial 2, an *observed* inter-trial repetition is scored. Once again, the final ITR score is obtained by subtracting from the observed repetitions the number which would be expected on the basis of chance alone. The ITR measure is, then, an index of the extent to which items are recalled in the same order on successive trials. If the superordinate-subordinate relation were the only one being employed by the subject, there is no reason to predict a high ITR score. For the subject would simply use the superordinate coding to retrieve the items which it subsumes in no particular order. It has been shown, however, that this is not the case. Higher clustering is accompanied by higher ITR scores, implying that the recall of one individual item can cue that of the next (Puff, 1970b).

Indeed, the presentation of the material in certain ways may result in the subject preferring a sequential strategy to a hierarchical one. For example, if items are presented in the same order on each trial, subjects tend to recall them in the same order; such presentation results in better recall than random-order presentation (Mandler, 1969). Further, if an item is added to the presentation list on each trial, most subjects employ a sequential strategy, even when the material is categorizable (Mandler and Dean, 1969).

We are left with the conclusion that the evidence for a simple reductive function of organization of a superordinate-subordinate nature is an artefact of the material selected and the measure employed.

5.3 The elaborative tradition

5.3.1 Order effects

One way in which subjects have been given more scope to organize is by presenting them with apparently unrelated words (Tulving, 1962). It has been found that when unrelated words are presented in a different random order on each trial in the multi-trial free-recall procedure, there are nevertheless con-sistencies in the order of their recall. These are indexed by the ITR measure. Degree of ITR and amount recalled tend to increase over trials, but are seldom highly correlated. Degree of ITR seldom reaches 50 per cent of the maximum possible. If ITR does measure the extent to which subjects organize unrelated items, then these findings are disappointing. For one would predict an increase in amount recalled whether the function of such organization is reductive or elaborative. However, the absence of reliable correlations and the failure of subjectively organized lists to resist interference may be due to the fact that the ITR measure is not an adequate measure of organization.

The presentation situation in a multi-trial free-recall task with unrelated words is a varied one. On each presentation trial a different order of items is presented. It is highly likely that subjects will encode items in relation to several other items, since the juxtaposition of different items on each trial would encour-age such relations to be formed. The relations could consist of simple position effects — each word being coded in terms of its immediately surrounding context. Or they could consist of the sort of overlapping of attributes described in 5.1.1, in which case an item could be coded in relation to several other groups of items. Either way, two items would not be expected to follow one another in the same order on each recall trial.

Postman (1972) makes a rather different point in criticizing the dependence of ITR upon the discrepancy between input order and output order. Clearly, any evidence derived from order of output that subjects are active upon the material must consist of differences between order of output and order of input. However, this methodological requirement rules out the possibility of discovering the extent to which subjects are using the order of items at presentation for coding purposes. Order of output may be the same as order of input because they are employing order as a coding device.

A final general criticism of the use of order of recall as an index of organization (whether in clustering or ITR measures) is that order of recall can be purely a performance variable (Colle, 1972). That is, one can instruct subjects to remember items in the same order over trials, and they may do so. However, recall is not improved. Therefore the use of the transfer methodology is considered preferable.

5.3.2 Transfer

The transfer task (Postman, 1971) does at least permit one to infer that any results are due to learning and not performance. In transfer paradigms, the effect of the learning of one list upon the learning of another is observed. However, the nature of the organizational learning involved has to be inferred from the effect of independent variables; it cannot be observed more directly, as in analyses of order of output.

The basic finding here is that of Tulving (1966) that part—whole transfer is negative. That is, given a list of unrelated nouns one half of which have already been learned, free-recall performance on that list is worse than if different unrelated words had previously been learned, at least on later learning trials; mechanical reading of the part list had no such negative transfer effect, however. If the words were being learned independently of each other, then prior familiarization with some of them would have resulted in positive, not negative transfer. Therefore one can infer that the words were being organized during part-list learning, and that this organization became inappropriate in the whole-list learning. The implication is that there was an optimal organization for the learning of the whole list. Further research has shown that whole–part transfer is also negative under the same conditions. However, when the organization of the part list can be carried over into the whole list, in the form of pairs of items or categories which are appropriate there, part–whole transfer is positive.

However, it must be stressed that there are alternative explanations besides the inference of a complex organization covering the whole list. Part–whole transfer might be negative because subjects may pay more attention to the new items in the whole list than to the old ones at presentation; further, they may recall the new items before the old ones, thereby subjecting the old items to possible interference; alternatively, this interference may be between codings of list membership, since the part-list members may have been tagged with list 1 membership, then list 2 membership (Bower, 1972a). It has indeed been found that old items are worse recalled than new ones. Whole–part transfer might be negative because subjects find it hard to discriminate in the part-learning between items which are in the part list and those that were in the whole list. More important, part–whole negative transfer may be a highly specific phenomenon, limited to material consisting of nouns. Hicks and Young (1972) showed that part–whole transfer was positive in the case of adjectives, and also that merely reading the adjectives of the part-list resulted in improvement in learning the whole list. Why should the effect be found with material consisting of one part of speech but not of another?

Other transfer research concerns the effects of paired-associate learning on subsequent free-recall learning. It was shown (Wood, 1969) that transfer is negative when one item of the associated pair is to be recalled in the free-recall task. The more members of the free-recall list that had been one of a pair, the greater the negative transfer. Thus the process involved in paired-associate learning appears to overlap with that involved in free recall. Otherwise, if entirely different processes were involved, there would be no interference. The same is true of Postman's (1971) consistent findings of negative transfer from free-recall to paired-associate tasks. In this case, it is inferred that the great majority of the relations by which material was encoded in the free-recall task are incompatible with the single arbitrary relation demanded by the paired-associate task.

5.4 Organization and association

5.4.1 Association

A great deal of discussion has centred on whether organizational or associational terminology is more appropriate for describing the results outlined in this chapter (see 1.4.1 and 1.4.2). As Postman (1968) notes, the basic criterion of any theory being termed associative is whether or not it contains the notion of contiguity in time. It is a cardinal tenet of associationism that events have to be experienced contiguously in time for the subject to code a relation between them.

It is evident that the typical free-recall task in which a list of items is presented can be conceptualized as a series of events (viz., the presentation of each item). It is clear that the order of presentation involves the contiguity of each item with the item preceding and succeeding it. Note has already been taken (5.2.3) of experiments in which consistent order of items at presentation has been utilized by subjects in their recall.

However, it is difficult to see how the principle of *explicit* contiguity can deal adequately with the recall of randomly arranged items in a principled order. The notion of *implicit* contiguity, on the other hand, can cope with these findings better. By implicit contiguity is meant functional as opposed to nominal order of input. Subjects may code categorically related items together even though they may have been presented scattered throughout a randomly ordered list (Wallace, 1970). One way in which such coding might be facilitated is by their consecutive rehearsal (Rundus, 1971).

Contiguity is a feature of the experimental situation. The knowledge of relations which subjects bring to that situation also has to be accounted for. Here again, associationists' emphasis has moved away from the assumption that items have to be *directly* associated with each other to the conclusion that they may be *indirectly* associated. Putting this operationally, it used to be assumed that for relations to be coded, the words concerned had to be associates of each other in the associative norms. Now, however, all association theorists suppose that two words may be related by the subject if they *share* common associates.

It has long been clear that *direct* associative relations between words in the list are not a necessary condition of organization. Bousfield, Puff and Cowan (1964) found that items of zero inter-item associative strength were nevertheless organized subjectively. Further, a computer programme based on direct inter-item associations (Bower, 1972b) failed to simulate the basic findings of (1) a correlation between clustering and recall, (2) negative part—whole transfer, and (3) Slamecka's (1968) work. Slamecka's finding is extremely important; he showed that the provision of list items as recall cues does not facilitate recall. This implies that items are not coded in terms of their *direct* association with other presented items.

The usually accepted alternative is that items are related to other items by means of the *implicit* word associates they share. This form of relationship may be conceived as chaining by means of sets of mediators; or it may be pictured as the activation of an associative network (Deese, 1966). In the latter case, words would be related if they belonged to the same portion of the associative network, i.e. if they shared a number of associates in common.

However, the associative approach may be criticized for its failure to take adequate account of the extent of the difference between nominal and functional stimuli. The notion of implicit *verbal* responses is based on the external *procedure* of requiring a verbal associate to a stimulus word. In terms of the theory of coding by attributes, however, a word might be given as an associate to another because it shares a certain number of syntactic and semantic attributes, as Deese himself argued. Free association data itself is merely a fact, not an explanation (Tulving, 1968).

Secondly, to explain organization of word lists in terms of implicit word associations is to limit one's explanatory powers. For one is thereby supposing that relations are coded by means of a certain limited type of attribute only. In fact, one is falling into the same trap as the users of the clustering measure, the trap of limiting the type of organization for which one is looking. In both cases, limitations of the measure and stereotyping of the type of material has resulted in a limiting of the scope of theory to certain very specific types of semantic relation.

Not only the *nature* of the relations has been limited by the experimental procedures, however. Also, the *functions* of organization have been seen in a simplistic way. The presentation of categorical material makes the inference of reductive coding obligatory. The invocation of the concept of implicit word associates inevitably means that many more events of the same form as presented items are coded than are presented. Thus the so-called organizational approach results in a purely reductive function, the associationist approach in a purely elaborative one.

5.4.2 Organization

This section will recapitulate some of the theoretical problems raised by the reductive approach. A major difficulty is to specify how the correct items are recalled. It is easy to see that a superordinate coding would result in the retrieval of items from the right category. It is noteworthy that Tulving and Pearlstone's (1966) cues at retrieval resulted in items from more categories being recalled, not more items per category. But unless one postulates individual coding of items as well as the coding of the superordinate relation, it is hard to see how the right as opposed to the wrong animals, for example, are recalled.

One way out of this difficulty has been to propose the existence of a recognition check (Kintsch, 1970a, b). Many animals might be retrieved, but only the correct few recalled, since a check is made on items retrieved to discover whether or not they were among the items presented. This, it is supposed, is why there are so few intrusions of extra-list items in normal recall protocols. Such a procedure, however, seems likely only when material is chosen from very well-known categories, and when the most common members of that category are the items presented; for then the subject has a fairly high chance of generating the correct items by means of the superordinate. The recognition check would not be over-burdened. Indeed, even if they have not been presented with any items at all, subjects can 'recall' the correct ones, given their category names (Cofer, 1966). In other types of situation, however, an impossible load would be placed on the proposed recognition check. When the relation coded is a fairly abstract one, a vast number of possible instances of it could be generated. It should also be noted that the idea of a recognition check implies that individual items must have been coded by at least one attribute — the fact that they had been presented.

A second solution to the problem for reductive organizational theorists of how to account for recall of correct items has already been mentioned. It is to suppose that items are coded individually, together with a retrieval plan which utilizes the perceived relation between items. The main proponent of this view has been Slamecka (1968). His finding was that individual items which had been presented were no use as cues at recall for other items which had been presented. He inferred that items were coded individually, since if they were coded in relation, such cues should be effective. However, the alternative explanation of these findings has already been proposed in 5.4.1, viz., that items were coded relationally, but not simply in terms of each other; item b was not simply coded as the item which followed item a. There is considerable other evidence to suggest that items are not coded independently of each other; the strongest such evidence is that of the negative transfer of part—whole lists. Moreover, there are many cases in which it appears to be necessary for codings at retrieval to be the same as those imposed at presentation (see 4.3.1). Furthermore, it seems very unlikely that items could be stored as independent traces when they are presented in the context of each other. Finally, relationships between items have to be perceived for the establishment of the retrieval plan; how could this occur without interaction of codings of the items concerned?

There is, however, another basic difficulty in the reductive organizational approach. It concerns the retrieval of relational codings. If each item is supposed to be coded under one superordinate coding, then the stored representation of the list has to be conceived of as a set of separate, unrelated superordinate codings. This is precisely the situation which could occur in the typical categorized list. A set of animals, a set of items of clothing, a set of the states in the United States, and a set of flowers do not appear to have a great deal of semantic overlap! Two ways out of this artificially induced dilemma have been proposed. Wood (1972) prefers yet higher order codings — an infinite regression? Others favour retrieval plans, with the consequent threat of the dreaded homunculus. The difficulty in all these cases, of course, is that of evidence. The provision of instructions to perform a recognition check, of 'super-superordinate' cues, or of retrieval strategies, may all prove effective. But this does not mean that subjects do habitually use these procedures, only that they can do so. The fact that they benefit from their provision may in fact imply that they do *not* habitually use such procedures.

5.4.3 Overlapping attributes

Early experiments were carried out in which degree of associative relationship between words and category membership were varied orthogonally (Cofer, 1966). This exemplifies the tendency to equate the nature of the material with the hypothesized processes. The two traditions outlined in this chapter derive from the same origins. Different types of material and different techniques of analysis have resulted in exclusive stress on one or the other function of coding, reductive or elaborative.

The advantage of the extensions of attribute coding to the multi-item situation is that it enables a unified explanation to be given for the apparently diverse findings of the two traditions. This is because it allows for both reductive and elaborative functions. Postman's (1972) rather gloomy conclusion, that different processes may have to be hypothesized to account for these findings, may be premature. Consider first the recall of typical categorizable lists. This is characterized by considerable clustering, by an increase over trials in number of items recalled per category, and by an increase in number of categories recalled as a result of the provision of retrieval cues. In terms of the attribute approach, these findings would be conceptualized as follows.

In the case of categorized lists, the relations between items are coded very early on in the presentation trials. This is because the attributes by which the items are related are very obvious. It is also likely that they will be very few in number — animals will be coded by an animal attribute (or perhaps more than one attribute: Henry and Voss, 1970). As a result of the rapid encoding of relations, the *number* of categories recalled will remain fairly constant over trials; as a result of the small number of attributes by which each relation is coded, individual categories may be inaccessible. Retrieval cues will be necessary to make their member items retrievable. The individual items, however, will become coded by more and more attributes over trials. As a result, the number of items per category recalled will increase gradually over trials.

In the case of unrelated lists, the typical results in the tradition have been the low degree of ITR obtained relative to the maximum possible; the low degree of correlation of ITR measures with recall; and negative transfer from part to whole and whole to part lists. In the coding of unrelated lists, there is no reason to think that codings of relations occur before codings of items. On the contrary, it seems likely that only when items have been coded by several attributes will any overlap of attributes between items occur. Overlaps may be multiple, in the sense that different relations may be coded for the same item. Thus the ITR measure will be inappropriate; it can only point to those relations which might exist between two particular items. Relations may extend over several items, and an item may be coded by several relations. If two items are recalled in the same order on successive trials, this probably indicates that the organization is *not* being used to aid recall. If it were, the use of several different overlaps of attributes as codings of relations would result in a different order of recall on each trial. Negative transfer is explicable in terms of the overlapping attributes being different for a part list than for a whole; different relations are consequently coded, and these codings of relations interfere with each other.

Thus the apparent discrepancy between the reductive and the elaborative traditions may be reconciled by the use of the notion of coding by attributes. The distinction between coding of items to distinguish them from each other and coding of relations by means of overlapping attributes has solved the problem for the reductive theorist of how individual items are correctly recalled. And the notion of overlapping attributes to code relations has provided the elaborative tradition with a reductive toehold. For networks of associations are purely elaborative, whereas the use of overlapping attributes to code relations makes it unnecessary for those attributes to be coded for each item.

Thus the findings typical of the two traditions are dealt with in terms of coding by attributes. The difference between the tasks of recall of categorizable and unrelated items is one of the order and number of the attributes by which they are encoded. In the case of categorical material, the attributes by which the items are related are coded very rapidly. They are few in number. The attributes which differentiate the items from each other are coded more slowly over trials. In the case of 'unrelated' items, both the overlapping relational and the differentiating attributes increase in number over trials, and there is no reason to think that the relational attributes are few in number.

5.4.4 Implications

The attribute approach is merely a framework, not a theory generating predictions. That is, its function is to lead to the asking of *certain sorts* of experimental questions rather than to point towards specific hypotheses.

Future research into organizational coding must start to ask the following sorts of question. Which attributes are employed for coding of relations, and under what conditions? What determines the relative proportion of overlapping (relational) and non-overlapping (item) attributes? What parts do relational attributes and item attributes play in the reconstruction of items from attributes?

The asking of these questions concerning the functional stimulus does not represent a departure from a commitment to empirical methods. The strictures of Postman (1972, p. 40) and Tulving (1968, p. 21) must be heeded. Postman says, 'Since organization is a theoretical construct, it is reasonable to suggest that the concept needs to be securely anchored to both antecedent conditions and observable consequences.' Tulving remarks, 'It seems more profitable at this time to start with the fact that certain words are more likely to be formed into clusters or S-units than others, and to ask what *intra-experimental* conditions determine the ease with which such S-units are formed.'

An example may be given of the sort of experiment required to answer these questions. The requirement is for *alternative* possible modes of organizing to be built into the material, and for task variables to be manipulated in order for their effect on the subject's choice to be observed. The strategy is therefore part-way between the use of material involving only one 'correct' mode of organization and the use of material permitting any sort of organization whatever. Mandler (1969) performed an experiment in which categorical material was presented over trials in the same order on each trial. Subjects were thus faced with the choice of using *either* semantic *or* positional attributes, as evidenced by the identity or similarity of order of items on successive trials.

A second example of the type of work required is the research of Horowitz and Manelis (1972). They investigated recall of adjective—noun pairs. Nouns were better recalled than adjectives and were better cues for recall of a pair. These results were explained in terms of the greater number of attributes possessed by nouns. Moreover, in some cases part only of the pair was often recognized, but in others, only the entire pair. In the latter case the adjective and the noun appeared to overlap in more attributes. These results did not obtain, however, where the pair formed a unit of meaning, e.g. 'hot dog', 'double talk'.

Finally, a connection with the previous chapter must be pointed out. The notion of levels of coding, elaborated in 4.2.1, is appropriate to organizational coding. The idea of levels of coding suggests that some coding attributes require less time than others, and are appropriate to different situations. Different experimental situations should therefore result in different types of attributes being employed for coding both items and relations.

5.5 Summary

It was argued that the situation in which multiple items are presented for recall must be analysed in terms of subjectively imposed (functional) units. Therefore the analysis of the coding of each item as though it were merely a separate event is mistaken. It was shown how two traditions of research have grown up. One emphasizes the reductive function of the coding of relations, the other the elaborative function. It was maintained that these emphases were the result of the material chosen for the experiment; they do not reflect essentially different types of coding.

The reductive tradition is characterized by a stress on the connection between the degree of organization (coding of relations) and amount recalled. A strong hypothesis, that the information processing system was limited to a strict upper capacity of seven units, was rejected. However, a weaker hypothesis, that amount recalled and degree of organization were positively related, seemed to be supported by the evidence. It was suggested that there is considerable evidence for the use of codings of relations being employed to retrieve items at recall. However, the fact that some items are not accessible at recall, although they are potentially available, suggests that coding is far from optimal. There is some evidence that organization has to be near optimal for recall to be benefited; it was hypothesized that where each item belongs to a single unit in a neatly packaged list, this improvement in recall was an artefact of the situation.

The elaborative tradition employs lists of apparently unrelated words. One method of indicating that the subject is organizing these items is to present the items in a different random order on each trial of a multi-trial free-recall task. It has been found that there are regularities over trials in order recall despite the variety of presentation orders. However, there are objections both to the type of measure of organization employed and to its use. An alternative method has employed the transfer paradigm. Negative transfer was found between previous learning of a part of a list and subsequent learning of the whole. It was concluded that items were coded in relation rather than individually, but the generality of these findings was questioned.

The use of the associative and organizational terminology to describe the results of the free-recall experiments was discussed. It was concluded that both were inadequate; the former because it resulted in explanations in terms of word associates, the latter because it permitted little active coding by the subject. An extension of the idea of attributional coding to the multi-item task was described, and it was shown that it could account for findings in both elaborative and reductive traditions.

CHAPTER 6

Semantic memory

6.1 Overlapping attributes

6.1.1 The concept of semantic memory

In previous chapters the variety of forms of coding which a subject imposes on material presented to him has been outlined. It has been suggested that the event of presentation itself is coded as an episode. Both the circumstances of presentation and the material presented are coded. It was maintained that sometimes information is coded automatically, while on other occasions it is attended to and consciously processed. In both cases, the products of the subject's prior experience and maturational development must be assumed to be responsible for the coding processes. The term semantic memory is employed to indicate that we need to characterize these products if we are going to arrive at an adequate explanation of how coding occurs.

The distinction between semantic and episodic memory is made most clear by Tulving (1972). He defines semantic memory as follows (p.386):

> Semantic memory is the memory necessary for the use of language. It is a mental thesaurus, organized knowledge a person possesses about words and other verbal symbols, their meanings and referents, about relations among them, and about rules, formulas, and algorithms for the manipulation of these symbols, concepts, and relations. Semantic memory does not register perceptible properties of inputs, but rather

cognitive referents of input signals. The semantic system permits the retrieval of information that was not directly stored in it, and retrieval of information from the system leaves its contents unchanged, although any act of retrieval constitutes an input into episodic memory.

The reader will at this point begin to equate the study of semantic memory with that of human psychology! Some sort of limitation of scope is necessary for the purpose of this text. The aim here is to characterize those features of semantic memory which must be hypothesized to account for the results of episodic memory experiments. Obviously, the episodic memory experiments themselves are one source of evidence for the nature of semantic memory; the different forms of coding evidenced in them indicate the variety of the material upon which semantic memory can operate. They do not, of course, necessarily show that different sorts of process, corresponding to different forms of coding, must be inferred. This chapter will also be concerned with other sorts of evidence than episodic memory experiments. These techniques include the tapping of subjects' knowledge by means of questions, their responses to the free-association task, their sorting of words or sentences into groupings, and their comprehension of sentences. All aim to reveal characteristics of semantic memory codes.

It was proposed in 4.1.1 that automatic coding taps codes in semantic memory directly. Therefore, as Posner and Warren (1972) suggest, tasks which result in automatic coding should be useful tools for the elucidation of these codes. However, it might also be argued that conscious coding is equally an aspect of memory process which requires explanation. Therefore the strategies involved in paying conscious attention to codings and transforming them further, for example, into images, are equally aspects of semantic memory. It will be suggested that these are differences of degree rather than of kind.

There is a great danger in treating literally metaphorical language about the *contents* of the semantic memory. One may use the metaphor of the dictionary, implying that an ordered set of words or concepts exists; or the metaphor of the computer, implying that a set of items of information is pigeonholed in a flexible and retrievable format; or the metaphor of a language, implying that sets of symbols and rules for their combination somehow exist in the head. Finally, one can speak of attributes and codes, as we have in this book, but all these are metaphors, and possibly somewhat dangerous ones. Their purpose is to contrast the more permanent characteristics of the products of prior learning with the processing of a particular piece of information at a point in time. This latter has been treated in process terminology for a long time — witness the information processing models. However, semantic memory, too, must be conceived in terms of process. The hardware of semantic memory is the brain — the mechanism necessary for its operation. The codes of semantic memory are best conceived as coding processes which are more likely to occur than other coding processes. The encoding and reconstruction of a sentence, for example, is a result of certain interpretative linguistic coding processes which are more likely to occur than others. Thus even attributes cannot be conceived as 'existing' in the mind. Rather, they must be thought of as the most atomistic way we have of describing process.

This chapter will also be concerned with *retrieval from* semantic memory. Retrieval from episodic memory depends on reconstruction of previously presented material. This material has been coded in terms of attributes of the presentation situation as well as of the material itself. Retrieval from semantic memory, on the other hand, requires reconstruction from attributes of the material only. In general, the research strategy is to provide the subject with certain attributes in an effort to discover which attributes and operations he uses and the order he uses them in. Once again, there is no reason to suppose that basically different processes are involved in the episodic and semantic tasks.

One final caution: research into semantic memory in the more strictly defined sense is a recent trend. Its techniques have been limited and material highly selective. Much work, for example, has concentrated on specifically denotative attributes of language, ignoring phonological, grammatical, affective and imagery components. Much of it has involved the comparison of individual nouns with each other, omitting other parts of speech and more structured discourse.

6.1.2 Method of comparisons
The notion of attributes and the overlap of sets of attributes has been at the heart of our attempts to explain some of the

phenomena of episodic memory. For example, the results of both the reductive and the elaborative traditions in the field of organizational coding were explained in terms of overlap of the attributes by which individual items were coded. In the former, the overlaps were made explicit by the experimenter, so coding of relations (i.e. coding of overlaps) was made easy. In the latter, overlaps were discovered and coded as coding of items progressed (see 5.4.3).

If one conceives of presented items being coded by bundles of attributes, then it should be possible to investigate the relations of these bundles of attributes to each other by presenting pairs of different items. One possible relation could be that of an hierarchical structure. The defining attributes of one term (e.g. animal) would differ from those of one of its closer subordinates (e.g. bird). In their turn, the attributes of 'bird' would differ from those of 'canary'. 'Animal' might be coded in terms of its living, moving attributes, 'bird' in terms of its flying characteristics, 'canary' by its yellow, singing attributes. The animal and bird attributes might not be required when the term 'canary' is being coded; a 'cognitive economy' principle permits these attributes to be retrieved when necessary by means of a traversing of the hierarchy.

To test this hypothesis, Collins and Quillian (1969) made subjects evaluate statements by indicating, as fast as possible, whether they were true or false. The statements ranged from 1.A 'canary is yellow' through 2.A 'canary is a bird' to 3.A 'canary is an animal'. Discovering longer reaction times for 'true' responses through 1 to 3, Collins and Quillian concluded that subjects had to traverse the hierarchy in 2 and 3. In other words, by forcing subjects to compare two terms (e.g. 'canary' and 'animal') at supposedly different levels in the hierarchy, they forced them to traverse a connection which included intervening concepts (e.g. 'bird').

One among the several possible alternative explanations, however, might run as follows (Schaeffer and Wallace, 1970). Subjects compared the two presented words directly by coding them into attributes and trying to find overlaps between the bunches of attributes. Such searches might take longer in the case of 'animal' and 'canary' than in the case of 'bird' and 'canary'. For the first few, or the most subjectively prominent, attributes into which 'animal' is coded might be quite different from those into which 'canary' is coded. However, 'bird' might share more prominent attributes with 'canary'. Therefore overlaps will be harder to find in the former case than in the latter.

Furthermore, any overlap discovered might be harder to evaluate. Evaluation is necessary to decide whether the overlap discovered actually evidences the relation required by the task. In this case, the task is to identify the superordinate-subordinate relationship. Only certain overlapping attributes will enable the instance 'canary' to qualify as a member of the category 'animal'. There is a certain combination of attributes which all animals have and only animals have. These are termed the defining attributes. The subject may accept a certain proportion of them as adequate evidence of 'animalness'. Only when he has discovered that these attributes form part of the overlap can he identify the item as an instance of a category.

To reject two terms as being not identifiable takes *longer* the closer they appear to be (e.g. it takes longer to deny that a daisy is a bird than it does to deny that gold is a bird). This reversal of the finding in the case of positively identifiable sentences is difficult to explain on the Collins and Quillian hypothesis. They have to suppose that subjects find more misleading connections in the hierarchy between more closely related terms. However, a far more reasonable assumption is that subjects take less time to decide that the two distant terms do not share any defining attributes in common. A daisy has the living attribute in common with a bird; the subject might code both words in terms of this attribute, and then have to search further before deciding that they have no further potentially defining characteristics in common. On the other hand, in the case of 'gold' and 'bird', the subject might run through the defining attributes (for him) of the two words (e.g. precious metal versus alive with wings); spotting no overlap he will decide that the two are not identifiable in the terms the task requires. However, other strategies are equally possible, and could equally well explain the results obtained.

When task characteristics are changed, these results are no longer obtained. Conrad (1972) discovered that the hierarchical relation was only evidenced when the task was one of saying whether or not an item was a member of a superordinate class. When the subject had to say whether items shared a common attribute or not, there was no difference when the apparent distance between items was varied. Incidentally, this study controlled for category size, a factor which probably confounded earlier results (Meyer, 1970). However, the major point is that different task variables can disrupt the hierarchy effect. Moreover, it takes just as long to decide that magnesium is not an animal than that it is not a dog (Collins and Quillian, 1970), and there is no correspondence between subjects' ratings of closeness of meaning of items and their closeness on the semantic hierarchy (Landauer and Meyer, 1972). Thus the 'cognitive economy' theory, with its formal hierarchical structure, is contradicted by the evidence.

6.1.3 Method of incomplete definitions

An alternative approach is to attempt to characterize overlaps between codings in a more general way. That is, one may judge that two words have similar codings, and try to discover which attributes are responsible for this apparent similarity. Miller (1972) has employed the method of incomplete definitions in order to try to discover these shared attributes. An incomplete definition is a substitutable phrase that has a more general meaning than the word it replaces. A dog can, like an elephant, be incompletely defined as a warm-blooded animal. Thus, while all dogs are warm-blooded animals, all warm-blooded animals are not dogs. Elephants and dogs share the common attribute (among others) of being warm-blooded animals. This could be partly the reason for their intuitive similarity.

Miller chose a set of 217 verbs for his analysis, all similar in that they were verbs of motion, involving a causative component (an actor does something) and a change of location. However, within this set, some subsets contained items which were more similar than others. He analysed these subsets to try to discover what the shared attribute was, an attribute which enabled him to group a subset together and differentiate it from other subsets of words. So, for example, he was able to distinguish a subset of motion verbs which involved travelling on land (as opposed to through water or air). Within this subset, he was able to make a further distinction, between travelling on land by foot and by other means. And within the sub-subset so formed, he distinguished various forms of walking (strolls, tiptoes) and running (sprints, jogs, trots).

It should be stressed that all these distinctions were made on an intuitive basis by the experimenter himself. However, the important distinction from the method of comparisons (6.1.2) is that they were made on the basis of an incomplete definition, a partial paraphrase. The partial paraphase was simply a phrase which came to mind in an effort to describe the similarity between certain items. It is, in other words, a subjective sample of the shared attributes, rather than an *a priori* assumption of what the defining attributes are. This method of paraphrase seems likely to be promising, since it directly taps our linguistic coding processes. As Liberman, Mattingly, and Turvey (1972, pp.307-8) say:

> We can see paraphrase, not as a result of forgetting, but rather as an essential condition or correlate of the processes by which we normally communicate and remember. This view, which we adopt, takes account of what seems to us quite evident: If linguistic communications could only be stored in the form in which they were presented, we should presumably be making inefficient use of capacity for storage and retrieval; the information must be restructured if that which is communicated to us by language is to be well remembered. Thus, the changes that are reflected in paraphrase include those that the separate processes of communication and memory require. Seen this way, the ubiquitous fact of paraphrase means that language is best transmitted in one form and stored in another.

Thus a paraphrase is apt to reflect the primary coding attributes we use.

However, an eminent psychologist's paraphrases might differ from those of others (if they did not in some ways, he might not be an eminent psychologist). Therefore a set of words was selected embodying the distinction exemplified above. The set was 'goes, rides, swims, walks, strolls, tiptoes, runs, sprints, jogs, trots'. Clearly these embody a variety of subsets, with 'walks, strolls, tiptoes' and 'runs, sprints, jogs, trots' being subsets within the subset 'travel on land by foot'. Each word was inserted in the verb position of the sentence 'John verbs to school'. Subjects then sorted the ten printed sentences into piles 'on the basis of similarity of meaning'. Any number of piles could be used. A co-occurrence matrix was drawn up, indicating the number of occasions when any one word was sorted with another. Results showed clearly that subjects sorted the two subsets of 'walking' and 'running' separately. However, 16 per cent formed a 'travel on foot by land' pile. 'Goes', 'rides' and 'swims' were occasionally sorted together, but mostly as isolated single unit 'piles'. Thus the paraphrase method which resulted in a 'travel on land by foot' subset was vindicated, and the additional intuition that 'walking' and 'running' were distinct was supported.

Similar analyses and sortings were carried out with other subsets. For example, verbs of directional motion can be paraphrased in terms of which direction they imply (visit e.g. to, turn e.g. around, descend e.g. down, and out e.g. withdraw). They can also be paraphrased in terms of whether they are objective (e.g. withdraw the needle) or reflexive (e.g. withdraw from the room). Subjects sorted into directional clusters, and within each directional cluster, between objective and reflexive. However, there were few occasions when different directional attributes were combined within an objective or a reflexive pile. Thus the directional attribute appears to be dominant.

By means of incomplete definitions, twelve different attributes were elicited for the 217 motion verbs selected for study. These attributes individually could not adequately paraphrase the distinctions which the experimenter could intuit, however. For example, 'travel on land' (medium attribute) was not adequate — the combination 'travel on land by foot at different speeds' (medium+instrumental+velocity attributes) was required. However, twenty subsets, defined either by single or by multiple attributes, were generated by the method of incomplete definitions and confirmed by sorting experiments.

Miller stresses that these results do not provide evidence as to how the subject has learned to code by attributes, as to how he does code in an episodic memory task, or as to how he understands or produces sentences using these attributes. His experiments are, he insists, studies of lexical memory. However, the usefulness of attributes in a generative way can be imagined. That is, one might use different ways of *combining* attributes to understand complex input or to produce complex output; Miller explicitly states that the attributes he isolated could be employed in many other semantic domains. Episodic memory (particularly memory for gist as opposed to verbatim memory) involves both these stages of coding (input and output coding).

Other researchers (Osgood, 1970; Fillenbaum and Rapoport, 1971), have investigated other areas of meaning. Osgood, for example, analysed exhaustively verbs referring to interpersonal behaviour. His method was to include the verb under analysis within different phrase or sentence frames. Then he would place different other words in the other positions in the phrase or sentence. Thus, for example, if the verb was 'ridicule', it could be placed in a phrase with the adverbs 'sincerely' and 'considerately', or with 'unfairly', 'meanly' and 'despicably'. Subjects were asked to judge whether, in ordinary English usage, the resulting phrases were acceptable or anomalous. By noting which adverbs were judged acceptable in combination with the verb in question, the experimenter was able to suggest the abstract attributes which underlay the verb. Factor analysis suggested the conclusion that the abstract attributes underlying interpersonal verbs were relatively few in number. They included associative≃ dissociative, self-oriented≃other-oriented, subordinate≃supraordinate, and future≃past. It should be noted, however, that the adverbs and verbs selected for the experiment were chosen on the basis of an *a priori* analysis of which attributes did underly interpersonal verbs.

6.1.4 Method of free association
The method of free association requires the subject to respond with the first word which comes into his head after being presented with a word by the experimenter. It thus has the advantage of permitting subjects to respond with any word they wish — it is largely free of the external context (Deese, 1970). As a result, of course, the subject may respond with words in all sorts of different relationships with the stimulus word (Kintsch, 1972). On the other hand, a more specific requirement by the experimenter (e.g. to respond with the first subordinate instance of the presented word that comes to mind: Battig and Montague, 1969) may be imposing the experimenter's view of how the relations between words may be coded.

The most important work on the structure of associative relations has been carried out by Deese (1966) (see also Pollio, 1968). He used single words as stimuli, required subjects to give single words as responses, and investigated the extent to which responses to particular words overlapped. Thus suppose fifty subjects were given nineteen words as stimuli, including such words as 'moth', 'insect', 'wings', 'bird' (Deese, 1962). One can estimate by means of a matrix the extent to which any of these words share common associative responses. So, for example, 'moth' elicited the response 'fly' from ten out of the fifty subjects, while 'insect' elicited the same response nine times. They did not elicit any other responses in common, however, except that they elicited each other for one and two subjects respectively. 'Wings' and 'bird' show much more overlap, however. From twelve and fifteen subjects respectively they elicited 'fly', from two and three 'feather', and from one and two 'flight'. Also, they frequently elicited each other. From these data, Deese calculated intersection coefficients between stimulus terms, which were essentially measures of the extent to which they had associates in common.

It is worth noting the variety of ways in which a group of stimulus words may be selected, according to Deese (1966, p.57):

> One of these is by the simple expedient of choosing words which are all frequently occurring associates of a given word, and then, in turn, finding the associates these words yield. Another way is to consider some structure capable of definition outside of associative terms, such as the sex-age structure — or the structure which would be implied by a kinship system. Associations obtained from such material will be organized, though the associative organization may not be precisely like the extra-associative structure which generated the table. In short, organized tables of associative meaning may be achieved by almost any method that takes advantage of the relations among concepts and words in a language.

Thus not only the task instructions but the criteria for selecting the stimulus ensemble are relatively unstructed. Nevertheless, sufficiently reliable results were obtained for Deese to be able to postulate two processes to account for associative overlap. The first is that of a sharing of common attributes of meaning. He suggests that the overlap of the associations to two stimulus words is a result of the overlap of attributes which those words share. Thus the technique of free association, like that of incomplete definitions, permits some guesses to be made as to the identity of attributes of meaning. For inspection and factor analysis of the associates which two or more words have in common makes certain hypotheses plausible. In particular, factor analysis makes it possible to decide which are the more basic attributes. For example, in the nineteen words chosen as stimulus terms in the experiment described above, a basic group of animate words emerges as having common associates (bees, flies, bug, wing, bird) and is distinguished from an inanimate group of words (sky, yellow, spring). Many of the more basic clusters of words can be described in terms of bipolar attributes in this way. Perhaps, like phonological distinctive features, the deep semantic attributes are bipolar in nature (see also M. G. Johnson, 1970).

The second basic process is that of contrast. Deese supposes that instead of grouping items together on the basis of several attributes, we sometimes select an attribute and contrast the position of different nominal items along it. This explains the frequent occurrence of antonym responses (hot≃cold), particularly in the case of adjectives. Such antonym responses might be expected to occur when one particular attribute of meaning is by far the most dominant in one's coding of a word. This seems seldom true of nouns, but more often of adjectives. The function of adjectives in discourse is possibly to enable the listener to decode the noun which the adjective qualifies primarily in terms of one particular semantic attribute. Therefore this difference in the nature of associative responses to words of different form class once again points to the subservience of grammatical to semantic attributes.

This interpretation of associations in terms of attributes has support from Deese's (1959) finding that items which were more likely to elicit each other as associates were better recalled in a free-recall task. This result suggests that overlapping attributes permit better coding of relations and hence better recall (see 5.4.3).

6.2 Rules for combining attributes

6.2.1 Perception of sentences

If the discovery of the regular ways in which we code material is the objective of research then we should consider tasks which require either coding of input or coding of output alone. That is, we should not limit ourselves to a consideration of episodic memory experiments, requiring both input and output coding. One such additional source of evidence is the research concerning the perception and comprehension of sentences — that is, research which aims to discover how subjects code sentences *at input*. The body of research which requires both coding of sentences at input and their reconstruction at output was reviewed in 3.2.3. It was concluded there that memory for sentences usually involved coding in terms of meaning. Consideration of the comprehension of sentences attempts to isolate part of this sequence; hopefully, we may learn from this analytic approach more concerning the processes by which coding occurs. Specifically, we may discover more about the *rules* for combining attributes in coding which enable rapid comprehension of sentences to occur.

A brief introduction to the nature of language coding was provided in 3.2.1. By way of recapitulation, the basic problem is to discover how the nominal stimulus of speech is coded into its functional linguistic meaning. And how, conversely, the attributes of meaning are constructed into an overt speech signal. The study of comprehension aims at discovering the former. The research is ably reviewed by Johnson-Laird (1974). Its results can be summarized roughly as follows: subjects appear to use all manner of different cues in no particular order in their efforts to code the sentence in terms of a meaning. As a greater variety of tasks has become used, the variety of the subject's procedures in reducing his uncertainty has become clearer. The basic inference that will be drawn from the data is that coding by means of all these different forms is aimed primarily at constructing an end product: a coding in terms of relations between semantic attributes. Thus comprehension tasks hopefully provide evidence of coding right down to the deepest level of meaning.

One type of task which does not require comprehension, but simply *perception*, nevertheless indicates that subjects habitually code sentences down to deep levels of meaning. Many experiments have presented subjects with a click at a certain point in a sentence. When subsequently asked at which point in the sentence the click occurred, subjects displace it. It is sometimes displaced to a boundary between underlying clauses, sometimes to a boundary between surface phrases. Whether the surface or deep grammatical structure (see 3.2.2) determines relocation of the click is a function of variables which have not yet been established (Chaplin, Smith and Abrahamson, 1972). The surface structure, of course, provides clues as to who or what is the topic of the sentence., and to what is being said about the topic; but these surface grammatical clues are not always reliable. In the passive voice, the surface structure subject is the logical object, for example.

This must not be taken to imply that surface grammatical features are coded first and deep features second as a check. Rather, both types of grammatical feature may be used in an effort to distinguish the underlying clauses. These clauses will correspond to some extent to the basic semantic coding. That is, the grammatical clause junction is a useful place to complete a portion of semantic encoding. For the clause may well describe one of the basic semantic elements of meaning, e.g. the actor. It seems likely that the length of a clause will determine how the subject divides the sentence up into sections for purposes of semantic processing. If the subject clause and verb are short, he may code them semantically together, and deal with the object clause separately (Martin, Kolodziej and Genay, 1971). Thus the reason why clicks are reported by subjects to have occurred at grammatical boundaries may be because these boundaries are points where the subject often completes a part of his semantic coding.

This interpretation implies that the listener is seeking to code sections of the sentence semantically as he hears it. Jarvella (see 3.2.3) showed that subjects only remember verbatim the immediately preceding clause in running discourse. Evidence to be presented in the next section suggests that coding of the first clause alone can reduce uncertainty as to what the meaning of the whole sentence may be. It is probable that in many situations, the listener will have hypotheses as to the semantic coding of the sentence before it is even started. These would be derived from its prior linguistic and non-linguistic context. Certainly, prior hints as to meaning facilitate or alter perception of sentences (Bruce, 1958; Rosenberg and Jarvella, 1970) and memory for passages of prose (Dooling and Lachman, 1971).

6.2.2 Comprehension of sentences

Ambiguous sentences seem to be coded by their two meanings, at least for part of their utterance. The sentence 'I like cooking apples' is a simple ambiguous sentence. Location of clicks by the subject is less accurate in the case of such sentences. It seems likely that subjects employ simultaneously two separate semantic codings until some disambiguating event occurs. Lackner and Garrett (1973) found that an attended ambiguous sentence in one ear could be disambiguated by a simultaneous sentence in the other ear, slightly softer. That is, subjects would reliably give one interpretation of the sentence rather than the other. Afterwards, subjects could not report the disambiguating sentence. They must have had both of the possible interpretations available 'while they were processing the sentence. Not afterwards, however, since it takes no longer subsequently to paraphrase ambiguous than non-ambiguous sentences. There is some other evidence that ambiguity is apt to disappear *during* the presentation of the sentence; for it is just as easy to complete an ambiguous as a non-ambiguous sentence, provided that the part given to the subject to complete contains a whole clause (Bever, Garrett and Hurtig, 1973). It is only when a subclausal part of the sentence is given that its ambiguity causes greater difficulty of completion. This implies that a semantic processing of clauses occurs, and that such processing is sufficient to permit the subject to hypothesize one semantic coding of relations rather than the other. The research on ambiguity, then, supports the notion of the use of codings of earlier parts of the sentence to construct a deep level semantic coding for the whole sentence.

Another technique for investigating comprehension is that of *verification* (Trabasso, 1972; Olson, 1972). Subjects have to say whether a sentence does or does not describe a state of affairs depicted by a picture. In other words, the sentence has to be coded semantically, then matched with a representation of the picture in order for a true≃false evaluation to be made. More grammatically complex sentences take longer to verify — passives, for example, take longer than affirmatives. This could be because it takes longer to code passives into their semantic form. However, other differences occur at the matching stage of the task. Specifically, true affirmatives are faster verified than false affirmatives — e.g. to verify that the sentence 'The girl is hitting the boy' is true, given a picture of the girl hitting the boy, is easier than to say that the sentence 'The boy is hitting the girl' is false, given the same picture. The reverse is true of negatives, however. That is, false negatives are easier than true negatives. So, given the sentence 'The girl isn't hitting the boy', it is easier to say that this is false, given a picture of a girl hitting a boy, than it is to say that the sentence 'The boy isn't hitting the girl' is true, given the same picture.

A popular theory (Clark and Chase, 1972) describes these

results in terms of truth tables. It is assumed that the subject starts off with a bias to match true with true; and that the affirmative form of the sentence is the basic form of which the negative is a derivation. Granted these two assumptions, it can be shown that the true negative is harder because it requires an extra change to the initial truth index. However, the reaction times upon which this theory is based may be confounded. For the act of encoding a negative sentence may itself increase the time taken to encode a picture (Krueger, 1972). Therefore the assumption that it is differences in the matching time only which are reflected in different verification times may be mistaken.

From the point of view of our present aims, the verification task has yielded a different sort of information from the perceptual and ambiguous tasks. It has been concerned with the evaluation of a semantic coding of the sentence against a criterion of truth value. They were concerned with how the semantic coding of the sentence was arrived at. The verification task requires conscious strategies, while the other tasks involved rapid automatic encoding along several dimensions (phonological, syntactic, semantic) in an effort to construct an appropriate semantic coding. The verification task required the use of formal rules in the shape of truth values. The other tasks required the use of rules in another sense: the listener must expect, recognize and code certain combinations of phonological, grammatical and semantic elements. In other words, he must have certain regular ways of constructing these combinations. These rules are limiting, in that only certain ways of combining elements are expected; but they are productive, in that new actual combinations can be formed (see 3.2.1). What is more important still, these rules appear to be so designed as to facilitate semantic coding by their very nature. Thus grammatical rules lead to the coding of elements of semantic meaning by enabling the subject to unitize the sentence. This unitization might be signalled on the surface, or might require some considerable depth of grammatical coding. The point is that it enables the subject to code to the ultimate semantic depth in an astonishingly short time. The speed of speech makes this a necessity.

6.2.3 Reconstruction from semantic memory
The previous section attempted to discover the ways in which sentences are coded into semantic attributes. The present section

aims at reviewing the evidence on how subjects reconstruct words from semantic memory — that is, how they derive words from attributes.

The research strategy employed in the investigation of the retrieval of items from semantic memory involves the experimenter providing the subject with certain attributes of a word. The subject has to respond as quickly as possible with a word which 'contains' those attributes. Retrieval in this sense thus actually involves producing a word. This technique contrasts with the techniques which require identification of an item as a member of a category. It was argued (see 6.1.2) that the latter in fact required comparison of sets of attributes rather than constructive retrieval.

Much of the research to be discussed employs the analogy of search through a store of words. It is assumed that the words of a person's native language in some sense 'exist' in an organized format. Therefore to ask the subject to produce a word from a particular category is to require him to direct his search to that category. And to ask him to produce a word of certain characteristics from a category (e.g. an animal beginning with the letter Z) is to ask him to scan the category until he arrives at an item of a subset which fits these requirements. These assumptions have led to the asking of questions concerning the nature of this supposed scanning process. If scanning is sequential, item by item, then retrieval from a larger category should take longer than retrieval from a smaller one (Landauer and Freedman, 1968). If, however, no such differences are found, then parallel processing must be hypothesized. This prediction is an analogue at the semantic level of the argument, at the level of visual recognition of letters, between proponents of parallel (e.g. Neisser, 1967) and serial (e.g. Sternberg, 1966) processing.

However, the evidence is confused enough to lead one to query whether in this instance the right questions are being asked in the right language. It is argued that it is mistaken to speak in terms of a lexicon or dictionary of words in the head. Instead, words should be seen as the behavioural products of construction by means of attributes. The construction of words as opposed to non-words has then to be explained in terms of previous learning of certain constructions; that is, of certain ways of combining elements.

Freedman and Loftus (1971) gave subjects the name of a

category (e.g. animal) and another attribute (e.g. the initial letter Z). The subject had to respond as fast as possible with a word which fulfilled these two criteria. The two factors varied were the size of the category (e.g. animals versus seasons) and the number of possible correct instances (e.g. animals beginning with Z versus proper names beginning with J). Neither of these variables had any effect on retrieval time. When the noun category was given before the letter name, reaction time was consistently faster than in the reverse situation. Freedman and Loftus interpret this result as indicating that the order of search is from category to subset, and therefore search cannot start until the category is specified. The results could equally well be seen in terms of the subject employing an order of types of attributes in construction — semantic, then phonological (see 4.2.3). The lack of effect of category size and of number of possible instances is interpreted as indicating parallel processing. However, it is equally possible that no search has to be undertaken — rather, construction has to be made. Other variables than category size would be expected to affect reaction time in this case. Specifically, subjects' familiarity with one or several of the possible responses is one such variable.

Subsequent findings appear to support this latter proposition. Loftus, Freedman and Loftus (1970) found that the time taken to retrieve a member of a category did not vary with category size (an example of an animal was given no faster than an example of a bird). However, reaction time *did* correlate closely with the word frequency of the most common category member. The more common a word is in the language, the faster it is likely to be retrieved. The same applies to the frequency with which an item is given as a member of the category (Loftus and Freedman, 1972). Furthermore, with frequency held constant, the earlier a word is acquired in development by children, the faster it is retrieved (Carroll and White, 1973). These findings imply that subjects construct words faster the more often they have constructed them before; they do not lend support to a search and scan procedure, where category size is the determinant of speed of retrieval, unless one supposes that more frequent words are at the top of a mental list. The interpretation in terms of attributes resolves the inconsistencies in results obtained. In the Freedman and Loftus procedure, the subject has to construct a word; in the Collins and Quillian procedure (6.1.2) he has to identify a word as being a category instance. In the former case category size has no effect, whereas in the latter it has. In the Freedman and Loftus procedure, there is no reason why it should be harder to construct a word from a large category than from a smaller, since it is the frequency of use of the attributes of the category name for construction which determine speed of retrieval of a word. In the Collins and Quillian procedure, the word and the category name are likely to have less attributes in common the more inclusive the category is (the further away from the word it is); therefore comparison time of sets of attributes will be longer the larger the category.

The attribute approach also resolves another apparent contradiction in the results. It will be recalled that when the task is to identify a word as being a member of a given category, positive identification that it *is* a member takes longer the larger and more inclusive the category. It takes longer to agree that a canary is an animal than that it is a bird. The reverse is true of *negative* identification, however. Consider now the results of a more recent experiment. Meyer (1973) found that when subjects had to say whether a word was a member of either of two categories, both positive *and* negative identification took longer the further apart the categories were. In the earlier research the word and the category name shared more attributes the smaller the category size and the 'closer' to the word; therefore there was more need to check further before deciding the word was *not* an instance. In Meyer's experiment the checking of the word's set of attributes against the first category name's attributes will facilitate its checking against the second if the two category names share some of the same attributes. Therefore both positive and negative identification will take longer the further away from each other the two categories are.

A different experimental technique also leads to results which suggest that the retrieval of words from semantic memory is a construction from attributes. This tries to explain the 'feeling of knowing' phenomenon in terms of the subject having constructed some of the attributes but not all. The 'tip of the tongue' experiment has already been quoted (see 4.2.4). The fact that subjects' feelings about how accurate they can be in recall or recognition tasks are very close to the mark has long been known. Their confidence ratings have been highly correlated with recall and recognition success (e.g. Murdock, 1965; Tulving and

Thomson, 1971). When there are certain items which subjects have failed to recall, subjects' feelings of knowing what these items are are related to their success in recognizing them when they are subsequently presented. This is true of words (Hart, 1967) and nonsense syllables (Blake, 1973). Moreover, when subjects cannot recall words with which they have been presented, they can still remember evaluative attributes of those words (Yavuz and Bousfield, 1956). However, all these results are derived from experiments of an episodic nature.

A technique more closely tapping semantic memory is that of Rubenstein, Garfield and Millikan (1970). They asked subjects if certain strings of letters were English words or not. Reaction time was faster to English words than to nonsense groups of letters, to high frequency than to low frequency words, and to homographs than to non-homographs (a homograph is a word with more than one distinct meaning). Rubenstein *et al.* explain these findings in terms of the dictionary search metaphor. They suppose that homographs have more 'lexical entries'. In terms of the attribute model, the presented letter strings would be coded in attributes, both phonological, syntactic and semantic. As soon as sufficient attributes had been coded to assure the subject that this was a word, he could respond. The greater speed of English over nonsense words would be explained in terms of all three types of attribute being available, of more frequent over less frequent in terms of practice in constructing, and of homographs over non-homographs in terms of the greater number of semantic attributes being available for the homographs.

Recent work tends to confirm this analysis. Meyer and Schvaneveldt (1971) made subjects make the same decisions (as to whether the strings of letters were English words or not) for two strings simultaneously. If the two strings were highly associated English words (bread≃butter), reaction time was faster than if they were not closely associated. This implies that coding by semantic attributes is important in the English versus nonsense comparison. Snodgrass and Jarvella (1972) carried the analysis a stage further. Using the English versus nonsense discrimination task once again, they varied the features of the words in a more refined way. The letter strings were made up of stems and sometimes affixes. The stems varied from English words (hard) through phonologically possible nonsense (dilt) to phonologically impossible nonsense (btul). The affixes were suffixes like '-ness' or prefixes like 'pre-'. Reaction time data showed that the reaction 'yes' to the English stem was faster than that of 'no' to the complete nonsense stem; the partial nonsense stem took longest. That phonological attributes *are* encoded is evidenced by the longer time spent over the partial nonsense. For 'dilt' can be given phonological attributes appropriate to those for a word. Therefore subjects must have taken longer to decide that they could not apply *all* the attributes which would qualify 'dilt' to be a word, since at least *some* of its attributes qualified it for word status. On the other hand, semantic attributes must also have been encoded very rapidly, since 'yes' to 'hard' was faster than 'no' to 'btul'. If phonological attributes were coded either first or only, this would not be the case. Finally, the affixes had an effect, suggesting that grammatical coding in terms of word class also operates in this task.

One final area of research suggests that retrieval from semantic memory follows the same principles as comprehension of sentences. When pauses in speech are investigated (Goldman—Eisler, 1968), it is found that the speaker pauses longest at the points of greatest uncertainty. One way of estimating degree of uncertainty is the guessing game — other subjects guess what the next word in the sentence is given a certain degree of previous context. Those words which are guessed worst are those with the greatest uncertainty. This finding parallels the comprehension findings that coding of an utterance is in terms of clauses which embody a certain group of semantic attributes in relation. Pauses imply breaks in construction just as clause boundaries are often points for breaks in coding for meaning.

In summary, construction of words and of sentences from semantic memory is probably in terms of attributes; just as in the case of the coding of input, it seems that subjects employ different types of attribute in no particular order. However, just as in the case of input again, it seems useful to talk about rules or regularities in the ways in which attributes are combined in construction. And it seems likely that construction in terms of semantic attributes is of primary importance.

A final point concerns the nature of the rules of combination. It is a matter of considerable doubt to what extent the psychological and the linguistic rules are similar. Many linguists aim at constructing abstract descriptions of language which are in the form of generative rules. These abstract rules have the aim of realizing all the acceptable combinations of elements in a language and none of the unacceptable ones. However, these formal axiomatic rules may well be different in kind from the probabilistic ways of coding by attributes which have been described in this book so far. On the other hand, it is quite possible that linguistic as well as psychological analysis will result in the discovery of the nature of the basic semantic attributes.

6.3 Inferences

Several forms of coding were mentioned in 3.2.4 in which subjects remembered the gist of a passage or a sentence. It was found that verbatim recall of running discourse was limited only to the immediately preceding clause; and that changes in meaning were subsequently recognized but changes in grammatical form were not; and thus it was concluded that paraphrase for meaning is the vital part of most memorizing activities where connected discourse is involved. It was also found typically that inferential reasoning occurred as part of the process of paraphrase. The experiments of Bransford showed that subjects subsequently falsely recognized expanded sentences as having occurred when in fact only portions of them had been presented. Also, that they falsely recognized consequences of presented sentences as having themselves been presented. Bartlett's famous work, of course, evidenced complete rationalization rather than isolated inferences.

That such inferences are a part of coding linguistic material is evidenced in many instances. To cite but two, the negative form of a sentence requires an inference if the intended meaning is to be understood from it. The sentence 'It is not a Collie' has to carry the inference that it *is* a dog (Kintsch, 1972). The negative implies an exception to a general rule, the existence of which has to be inferred before its negation in a particular case can be understood (Wason, 1965). As a second case consider pronominalization, the use of a pronoun to stand for a noun. There are many cases where an inference has to be made before the listener can determine which of two nouns the pronoun is referring to (Winograd, 1972) — for example, 'The boy fed the dog a bone, but it wouldn't eat it', and 'The boy fed the dog a bone, but it didn't suit it'.

Kintsch (1972) asked subjects to state what the clear

implications of certain sentences were. In many instances, subjects responded by supplying a missing grammatical case. For example, to the sentence 'Seymour carves the turkey', many subjects responded by supplying the instrumental phrase 'with a knife'. However, there were also many more general implications. The implication of 'The book was printed' was stated by several to be 'Someone wrote the book', of 'Cecil continued eating' to be 'He was eating before', of 'Gladys was blackmailed' to be 'She had a guilty secret', of 'Leo suffocated' to be 'There was a lack of air' and 'He's dead'. It seems that in many cases our coding of relations between sets of attributes goes beyond the relationship apparently expressed by an utterance.

If there is an intimate connection between our coding of linguistic events and of the non-linguistic context of their utterance, then it is easy to see how this type of inference could occur. The context in which the sentence 'Leo suffocated' was uttered could only be the context of a dead Leo. However, we often make inferences when we have never experienced the non-linguistic context. Our coding of the sentence might in fact depend on the coding of the word 'suffocate' in terms of its consequence normally being death. Our previous experience of the word in the verbal context 'Suffocate to death', or in the context 'Nearly suffocated' (used of a person still alive) may have resulted in this particular form of coding. Given that 'Suffocated' may be coded in this way, then the coding of the sentence 'Leo suffocated' will involve the relation of the attributes of Leo and of death. The inference of Leo's death from the sentence 'Leo suffocated' is therefore explicable in terms of coding of relations by means of attributes. A similar explanation can be offered for Bransford's finding of a sentence being coded in terms of its effect. One does not need to suppose that the subject performed a logical operation to draw the inference.

The same argument applies to the inferences considered necessary for the supposed working of the cognitive economy model of Collins and Quillian (see 6.1.2). If 'canary' is to be identified as an animal, it is supposed, then the inferential chain 'canary is a bird, birds are animals, therefore canary is an animal' must be followed. Once again, it may be argued that the identification of 'canary' as an animal is in fact a comparison of codings, that the codings of 'canary' and 'animal' have less attributes in common than those of 'canary' and 'bird', and that therefore comparison time and evaluation time will be longer for the former than the latter.

In general, it may be concluded that the codings of any particular word or phrase may well be in terms of the codings of the linguistic and non-linguistic events which have been its context in the prior experience of the subject. Therefore the juxtaposition of two such words in a sentence may well involve a relationship being coded which is not strictly speaking expressed by the utterance. However, there is danger in assuming that there is a 'correct' or strict definition of a word's or a sentence's meaning. The meaning is how the speaker and the listener code the utterance. In some cases, e.g. 'Leo was buried yesterday', the speaker *intends* the listener to make the inference the (unless he is an escapologist) Leo is dead. In other words, 'making inferences' is probably part of the normal coding of utterances. A formal logical process does not have to be postulated to account for this sort of coding. Rather, the explanation is to be found in the semantic attributes into which individual words can be coded; and hence in the variety of relations which can be coded when the words are placed together in an utterance.

6.4 Summary

It was argued that the concept of semantic memory is necessary in order to emphasize the fact that to any episodic memory task the subject brings the products of his previous experience. The efforts to characterize these products are limited and fragmentary in nature. Attempts to establish a hierarchical structure as the best description of these products were described. However, it was concluded that these attempts to establish a principle of cognitive economy whereby words need not be coded by the attributes of their superordinates have not yet succeeded. The manipulation of task variables has shown the experimental effect to be fragile; furthermore, the results can just as easily be described in terms of comparison of sets of attributes as in terms of retrieval from a hierarchy.

The use of various other methods in the attempt to characterize semantic memory was also described. Both the method of incomplete definitions combined with subjects' sortings and the method of free association suggest that underlying the groupings of words which subjects produce are abstract semantic attributes of meaning. These attributes may sometimes be binary or bipolar in nature. Subjects' groupings can be explained in terms of combinations of several attributes.

However, none of these studies suggests the ways by which attributes are combined to encode or construct the nominal stimulus or response. The comprehension of sentences was considered one method by which the coding of input into its semantic attributes could be investigated. It was suggested that the coding of other attributes of sentences — for example, their grammatical structure — assisted the coding of sentences into their semantic meaning. Specifically, results from studies of the perception of sentences and the comprehension of ambiguous sentences suggest that subjects segment sentences into clausal units and encode these separately in terms of their meaning. It was suggested that subjects code incoming sentences in such a way as to form hypotheses about what the intended meaning of the sentence is before it has been completely uttered. It was proposed that subjects have expectations about the regular combinations of phonological, grammatical and semantic attributes. These regular ways of combining attributes were termed rules, but it was stressed that these rules and the generative rules proposed by linguists were likely to differ in nature.

The investigation of the construction of words from semantic and other attributes was also reviewed. It was concluded that the frequency of words in the language (that is, the practice which the subject had had in constructing those words from their attributes) was a major determinant of retrieval speed. It was also concluded that these results made it difficult to conceive of semantic memory as a lexicon from which words are retrieved. It was argued that the correct metaphors are process (coding and construction) rather than content.

The fact that memory for sentences involved paraphrase was stressed. It was argued that paraphrase necessarily involves inference, and that inference can be characterized in terms of the overlapping of the varied semantic attributes by which words can be encoded.

No consideration was given to the way in which semantic memory might change. In order to do justice to this topic, the whole field of cognitive development and learning would have to be reviewed. Furthermore, no attention has been given to the conscious use of reasoning processes, although obviously these throw considerable light upon semantic memory.

CHAPTER 7

Past, present and future

7.1 Recent historical perspective

7.1.1 Interference theory

The language predominantly used in experimental psychology prior to 1960 or so was that of stimuli, responses, and the learned associations between them. Memory performance was therefore seen as the product of learning — could one on a subsequent occasion produce a response to a stimulus having learned the association between the two on a previous occasion? When it became clear that there were many occasions when one could not, this fact required explanation. For, given the paradigm of learning theory, the non-availability of a response once learned is something which has to be explained. Therefore the early emphasis was on forgetting rather than remembering, and the basic technique was that of paired-associate learning.

Two early concepts in the effort to explain forgetting were those of decay and interference. (For an introduction to interference theory see Cermak (1972), and for comprehensive reviews of interference theory and research see Postman (1969) and Postman and Underwood (1973).) In brief, interference theory is based upon the idea that preceding or subsequent events interfere with one's memory of the to-be-recalled material. A typical retroactive interference design has subjects learn paired-associate list A, learn B, have a certain period of time out, recall A. A proactive design has subjects learn B, learn A, time out, recall A. Control groups have no task B.

It was found that while proactive interference had the same effect whatever the time out, retroactive interference had a lesser effect after forty-eight than after five hours; that is, there was recovery (Underwood, 1948). This suggested that there was something specific about the retroactive design (in which subjects learned the interfering material *after* they learned the to-be-recalled material). This specific something was termed unlearning. Thus in addition to the possibility of response competition between the products of the two learning tasks, there was also the possibility of the unlearning of the first list while the second (interfering) list was being learned. It was assumed that this unlearning effect dissipated over time, however, since performance was the same under both retroactive and proactive conditions after forty-eight hours.

It was considered that unlearning might be considered the specific extinction of list A responses during list B learning. That is, list A responses might occur, but would be incorrect. However, encouraging subjects to make more (incorrect) list A responses during list B learning did not result in greater retroactive inhibition. It was therefore concluded that a more likely explanation for unlearning was inability to distinguish the two sets of responses. Thus after a few trials of learning list B, list A responses still intervene a lot. But on later trials few list A responses occur because the subject has learned which *set* of responses is appropriate. This explanation is supported by findings that the more similar the responses are in list A and list B, the greater the retroactive interference. This could be because the sets of responses are harder to discriminate as a result. Thus explanations of retroactive interference have moved from the extinction of a stimulus—response association to the failure to discriminate lists. Ways in which lists may be coded and therefore discriminated have been described in 2.5.3; most of the forms of coding which discriminate lists from each other are episodic in nature, being based on the different circumstances in which they were presented.

If interference is to be postulated as an explanation for forgetting *in general*, however, then it has to be shown that general habits of a linguistic nature interfere with material of a linguistic type. After all, the historical antecedent of interference theory was Jenkins and Dallenbach's (1924) study which showed that subjects who slept during the presentation—recall interval recalled more than those who went about their daily tasks. Many experiments have been carried out in an effort to show that, for example, high frequency words are less well remembered than low frequency words over a period; this would be hypothesized on the basis that they would elicit more associates which could suppress the word itself; recovery from such suppression would be predicted, however, over time. Unfortunately for the theory, neither differences between material of differing frequency nor spontaneous recovery over time have been reliably found. One way out is to suppose that degree of meaningfulness has two opposite effects. One is that predicted — that with materials of high meaningfulness, a lot of competing alternative but incorrect responses are elicited by the stimulus terms of the paired associates at recall. The other is the effect which has dominated our explanations of the functions of coding: the capability of a word to elicit many associates implies that it can be coded by several common attributes of meaning. These elaborative codings should help towards retrieving the correct item. Thus failure to obtain predicted results may be due to two effects working in opposite directions.

The attempt to explain forgetting in terms of the acquisition and extinction of associations has clearly been a failure. The explanations that have gained popularity, list differentiation and the influence of language 'habits', are, of course, consonant with the coding hypothesis; and the failure of the predictions based on the interference of language habits is due to an underestimate of their possible beneficial functions.

7.1.2 Techniques of short-term memory research

A major alternative explanation of forgetting was in terms of the decay of the memory trace over time. The basic strategy of proponents of the decay theory was to demonstrate that subjects forget material even when little opportunity has arisen for interference to occur. One way of ensuring such a situation was, it was thought, to demand recall very soon after presentation. A range of short-term memory tasks was therefore devised, characterized by their short presentation—recall interval and the small amount of information presented to the subject. This latter feature was considered necessary because it was thought that when a considerable amount of information was presented, interference between items could occur.

The first task employed the distractor technique (Brown, 1958; Peterson and Peterson, 1959). The subject is presented with a small amount of information, e.g. a triple consonant CCC nonsense syllable, a CVC nonsense syllable, a three-digit number, or three common words. These are removed after, usually, two seconds, and then immediately the subject has to commence an unrelated task, e.g. counting backwards in threes from a number given him by the experimenter. Then, after a certain length of time, up to about twenty seconds, the subject has to recall the material. Performance deteriorates in a negatively accelerating function, until by eighteen seconds a few subjects can recall any of the material. The subjects were prevented from rehearsing by means of the interpolated task, so their performance is taken as an index of 'pure' forgetting. This forgetting was assumed to be due to decay over time of the memory 'trace'.

However, subsequent research (Keppel and Underwood, 1962) showed that proactive interference operated in this situation, with previous trials proactively interfering with performance on later trials. The degree of proactive interference was shown to be a function of number of previous trials, i.e. of number of preceding items (different items were presented on different trials, since the task is essentially a one-trial task). It also occurred as a function of degree of similarity of items, since, as Wickens, Born and Allen (1963) showed, presenting material of a different class resulted in release from proactive interference (see 3.1.2).

A second important technique is the probe-digit technique, first employed by Waugh and Norman (1965). This involved the presentation of lists of sixteen digits. The last digit had occurred before in one of several positions throughout the list. When it occurred a second time (in position 16) a high-pitched tone signalled to the subject that it was the probe. He had been instructed to respond to the probe by reporting the digit which had followed it when it had been presented earlier in the sequence. The purpose of the probe technique is to prevent proactive interference on recall of subsequent items by recall of previous items. The digits were presented at the rate of either one or four per second, and it was found that this variable had no effect on recall. Now if performance had been worse when presentation was slower, this would have pointed to decay. On the other hand, performance on later digits was considerably worse than that on earlier ones, implying proactive interference.

A third technique is that of Conrad (1964), who presented fewer (six) items at a fairly fast rate and required correctly ordered recall of all of the items. His results showed the effects of acoustic interference (see 2.3.1).

In the case of all of these techniques, very large losses of information occur over very brief periods of time. Such results seemed to support the decay theory. Melton (1963) made a powerful attempt to incorporate the STM findings into interference theory, arguing that in most of the STM tasks, parts of the stimulus interfered with other parts (e.g. different letters within a CCC trigram interfered with each other). Despite Melton, however, a commonly held view was that LTM forgetting was caused by interference, STM forgetting by decay. The way was therefore paved for a distinction between STS and LTS — that is, for an inference about the structure of the memory system. However, as will be seen in 7.2.2, it soon became evident that interference was operating in STM tasks; but it was supposed, with Baddeley (1972a), that the interference in STM was at an acoustic level, that in LTM at a semantic level. In summary, then, alternative ways of explaining all forgetting became separate ways of describing forgetting in different situations. When this generalization in its turn failed to account for the evidence, different sorts of interference were supposed to be operative in the two types of task. As will be shown, this final generalization has also itself been overtaken by the evidence.

7.2 The modal model

7.2.1 Serial position effects

Most current models of memory make the distinction between STS and LTS, so that Murdock (1972) appears to be justified in calling it the modal model. Perhaps the best-known form of the modal model is that presented by Atkinson and Shiffrin (1968), although earlier exponents were Waugh and Norman (1965). Its essential features are: the notions of a sequential passing of information from STS to LTS; the limited capacity of STS as opposed to the essentially unlimited LTS; and the process of rehearsal as a means of transferring information from STS to LTS.

Instead of reviewing each of several closely related theories, we will first consider the essential part of them all (the STS versus LTS distinction) and the most convincing evidence for this distinction (serial position effects in free recall). Glanzer (1972) provides a thorough and well-argued review of this evidence, which, it must be stressed, is some of the most reliable empirical work in experimental psychology. The serial position curve is obtained by plotting the probability of a particular item being correctly recalled along the ordinate, and the item's position in the sequence of items presented along the abscissa. The important features of the curve obtained by this method are, firstly, its asymptote. That is, we are interested in discovering the degree of probability of recall of those items which occur in the positions at which the curve levels out. Typically, there is a primacy effect — subjects are more likely to recall the early items of the series; and there is a recency effect — the last few items are also better recalled. The asymptote is reached with the middle items; the longer the list, the more items fall along the asymptote (Murdock, 1962). In other words primacy and recency effects are limited to the first and last few items of the list, however long it is.

The crucial evidence concerns the interaction of independent variables with serial position. Several variables have been shown to affect the asymptote, but very few the recency effect. For example, the higher the rate of presentation, the lower the asymptote: middle-of-the-list items are worse recalled the faster items are presented (Murdock, 1962; Glanzer and Cunitz, 1966). Second, the more items in the list, the lower the asymptote (Murdock, 1962; Postman and Phillips, 1965). Third, the lower the degree of associative relatedness between items, the lower the asymptote (Glanzer and Schwartz, 1971). Finally, the less frequent the words presented are in the language, the lower the asymptote (Raymond, 1969). None of these variables has any effect on the recency portion of the curve, which remains essentially the same. Glanzer (1972) concludes that, since the variables have differential effects on different parts of the curve, then different structures are implicated. Specifically, the primacy and asymptote performances 'reflect output primarily or wholly from LTS . . . the last few positions reflect output from both STS and LTS, with the STS dominant' (p. 134).

There are, on the other hand, one or two variables which affect the recency portion of the curve but not the asymptote.

Specifically, when a distracting task is introduced at the end of the presentation of the list, the recency effect in recall is wiped out; last items are no better remembered than middle items (Glanzer and Cunitz, 1966). Thus the recall protocol in such cases is taken to reflect output from LTS only; output from STS alone can be calculated using formulae which, essentially, correct the recency effect for a possible continuing LTS component (Craik, 1971).

The inference of two stores is not the only inference made from these results, however. The information processing model is seen as a flow diagram, with information being *transferred* from STS to LTS. Thus the asymptote reflects the modal rate of transfer of information, and the effect of increased rate of presentation in depressing the asymptote is taken to reflect the difficulties of transfer at a high speed to LTS. Further evidence has to be provided that demonstrates this transfer function of STS. One such piece of evidence relates to the factors which result in removal of items from STS. If the distractor task between presentation and recall is varied, the specific factors which are responsible for the removal of items from STS may be discovered. They may be inferred from the discovery of which variables affect the recency effect. Neither the information load (counting backwards in ones, threes or sevens) nor the similarity of the intervening task to the to-be-recalled material appears to affect the recency effect (Glanzer, Gianutsos and Dubin, 1969); these variables, on the other hand, do affect the asymptote (Murdock, 1965). One variable which affects the recency effect is the *number* of words in the intervening task. The presentation of five or six words can completely erase the recency effect; of fewer, partially (Glanzer, Gianutsos and Dubin, 1969). Therefore, it is argued, the mechanism of STS is *displacement*: that is, there is a limited total capacity to STS, and incoming items 'bump out' earlier presented items.

The results quoted above have been obtained using the free-recall paradigm. Glanzer (1972) reviews evidence in an attempt to show that the same sort of serial position effects may be obtained with the other techniques. With probed recall of paired associates, Murdock (1963) found the expected inter-action of serial position with rate of presentation and with number of items presented. In the case of fixed-order serial recall, the subject has to recall the later items after having recalled the earlier items. In other words, recall of the earlier items is an interpolated task, as it were, which should remove the recency effect. This is what happens, provided the subject is forced to start recall immediately presentation is stopped. Otherwise, he uses a period after the last items have been presented to rehearse them before he starts his recall (Jahnke, 1968a, b). Thus some other STM tasks appear to confirm the STS versus LTS distinction as evidenced by the serial position curve.

7.2.2 Other evidence

Further grounds for distinguishing between STS and LTS are provided by Baddeley (1972a, b). One additional variable which he suggests has differential effects on STS and LTS is similarity of items. Baddeley maintains that, in general, acoustic similarity within the material affects STS but not LTS, semantic similarity the reverse. He suggests that when strict definitions of STS and LTS in terms of asymptote and recency are adhered to, differential effects are obtained. The evidence does not seem to support this proposal. While the early evidence upon which the generalization was based employed STM tasks, there is no indication that the effect of acoustic similarity was on STS (see for example, 2.3.1). Those experiments which do seem to support the generalization, and which at the same time distinguish STS and LTS effects properly, mostly use the probe technique. Levy and Murdock (1968) found that whole lists of acoustically similar words produced less of a recency effect than acoustically dissimilar words — i.e. acoustic similarity (and hence confusability) reduces the amount held in STS. Kintsch and Buschke (1969) obtained the same result for lists in which pairs of words only were acoustically similar. Thus the influence of acoustic similarity on the recency effect is strongly evidenced.

On the other hand, there are many experiments which do not support Baddeley's generalization. Firstly, experiments not distinguishing STS from LTS by the serial position curve, but nevertheless demanding extremely short-term recall, show semantic effects (see Wickens, 3.1.2; Shulman, 1972, and 4.2.1). Second, various other techniques besides the probe technique show opposite effects. Bruce and Crowley (1970), for example, using free recall, found both acoustic and semantic effects on recall even when there was a considerable interval between presentation and recall which effectively confined the result to LTS. Craik and Levy (1970) found both acoustic and semantic effects on asymptote, with both types of similarity increasing recall; they also found that semantic similarity decreased the recency effect. Even the probe technique itself shows that acoustic similarity can have an effect on the asymptote and not on the recency effect (Bruce and Murdock, 1968). To draw together all these findings, Glanzer, Koppenaal and Nelson (1972) found that both acoustic and semantic similarity affected both asymptote and recency effects, thus conclusively demonstrating that if STS and LTS are to be distinguished, the distinction cannot be based on the type of information held.

Thus differential effects of similarity of material may not be cited as evidence for an STS versus LTS distinction (Shulman, 1971). Baddeley (1972b) replies, however, that in those experiments where semantic coding was evidenced in STS, this was in fact due to the subject's utilization of rules of a semantic nature stored in LTS to retrieve acoustically coded material from STS at recall.

Another argument in favour of the distinction concerns the identity of the units processed in STS and LTS. It has been suggested that the word may be the basic unit in STS. Tulving and Patterson (1968) presented four highly related words (e.g. north, south, east and west) as part of a list of unrelated words in a free-recall task. These were remembered better when they were presented in the middle portion of the list than at the end or randomly throughout. More chunks were recalled, also. Tulving and Patterson explained the results in terms of retrieval processes. However, supporters of the STS versus LTS distinction would interpret them in terms of STS storage being of the articulatory-acoustically coded words, LTS of the semantically coded functional units (chunks). Craik (1968) showed that words could vary in length without having any effect on the recency effect. Thus the identity of the word as 'the' unit in STS, with the attendant stress on its articulatory-acoustic features, was attractive. However, smaller units than the word (Murdock, 1962) and far larger units such as proverbs (Glanzer, 1972) have also been shown to exhibit the recency effect. Therefore it seems reasonable to conclude with Craik (1971) and Glanzer (1972) that 'the' unit is whatever unit the subject codes the material into. Glanzer prefers to speak of 'any item that is in the subject's lexicon'. Thus there is no evidence in terms of the nature of the unit processed which justifies an STS versus LTS distinction.

A third type of evidence upon which an STS versus LTS distinction is based is neuro-physiological. Reviews of disorders of memory are provided by Talland (1968) and Warrington (1971). Essentially, this evidence consists of cases where brain-damaged patients appear to have normal STS but impaired LTS function, or vice versa. The earlier tests of STS function on which these generalizations are based, however, were often those of auditorily or visually presented digit-span tasks as employed in standard tests of intelligence. In essence, these are serial recall tasks, and, as has been suggested already, the major component in these tasks is LTS if the serial order phenomenon is the strict criterion. Baddeley and Warrington (1970), however, using the distractor technique, found no greater effect on certain amnesic brain-damaged patients than on normal controls. Further, while comparable recency effects for the two groups were obtained in free recall of ten-word lists, the brain-damaged patients had a lower asymptote. Thus LTS but not STS seems to be impaired.

Other patients, however, exhibit STS impairment only. Using the digit-span technique, Warrington and colleagues discovered patients who had an auditory digit span of one, although, contrary to the usual modality effect (2.4.1), their visual span was longer. Using a free-recall task, it was found that these patients showed much reduced recency but normal asymptote effects (Shallice and Warrington, 1970).

For the first type of patient ('impaired LTS') Warrington proposes that their difficulty is in fact one of retrieval. For provision of a recall cue consisting either of a partial visual representation of the words or of their first three letters resulted in essentially normal recall of eight-word lists. Such cues clearly reduce the number of possible alternatives for retrieval.

Since amnesic patients with LTS impairment do have the ability to code relations, Warrington concludes that their difficulty in retrieval is due to an inability to inhibit retrieval of other stored information.

With regard to the patients with impaired STS but normal LTS, Warrington (1971) suggests that 'these findings indicate that information need not be transferred from STM [=STS] to LTM [=LTS], as is commonly assumed, but that the two systems can function in parallel' (p. 247). How otherwise could these patients have recalled at an asymptotic level typical of normals? Obviously, this finding throws grave doubt on the notion of a sequence of processing, with information being passed from STS to LTS; it argues, on the contrary, for direct entry into LTS.

Therefore the evidence for the STS versus LTS distinction based on findings other than the serial position curve effect for normal subjects seems less strong than appears at first sight.

7.3 Rehearsal

7.3.1 Rehearsal as an active STS

There is considerable evidence which suggests that STS cannot be conceived of as a static store into which additional items are entered which 'bump out' earlier items. On the contrary, it seems clear that it must be considered an active process rather than a passive store. For certain variables other than simply number of items filling a container of a limited capacity have recently been shown to affect the recency effect. First, it has been shown that repetitions of the same item one after the other do not have any effect on STS capacity as measured by the recency effect (Glanzer and Meinzer, 1967; Waugh and Norman, 1968). This implies that the repetitions are recognized for what they are, and filtered out. There must, therefore, be a control selection process operating; not all input is processed through STS.

Second, Gianutsos (reported in Glanzer, 1972) has found that presenting words grouped in threes as opposed to at a steady rate has an effect on recency as well as on the primacy effect. When overall rate is faster, the superiority of grouped over steady presentation increases. This implies that material can be grouped in STS, Glanzer concluded. Glanzer's finding that proverbs can act as units in STS (7.2.2) also implies a grouping analysis, this time in terms of meaning. Thus if the recency effect is taken to be an index of the material in STS, and if the units in STS are sometimes functional rather than nominal, it follows that any rehearsal process the function of which is to transfer material from STS to LTS cannot deal only with nominal items.

Atkinson and Shiffrin (1968), however, treat rehearsal as a control process with two apparently contradictory functions. The first is to recirculate nominal or acoustically coded items into STS to prolong their existence there (Broadbent, 1958).

Such recirculation is required because of the limited capacity of STS, they argue. This recirculation may well involve overt or covert utterance of the item; indeed, Morton (1970) identifies it as a feedback loop between the word store of the subject and his speech motor apparatus. However, the maintenance of the material need not be in terms of its acoustic-articulatory attributes; rehearsal of visually coded material may occur (see 2.2.3).

The second function of rehearsal suggested by Atkinson and Shiffrin is to permit material to enter LTS. Evidence that subjects can specifically use verbal rehearsal to do so has come from studies by Rundus (1971). He found that forcing subjects to rehearse aloud after each item, *presented at a slow rate,* improved recall, having its effect on the asymptote and not on the recency portion of the curve. He also found that subjects rehearsed together categorically related items which were not presented together, implying the use of rehearsal to actively group items. Bjork (1970) also shows that the opportunity to rehearse in between presentation and recall results in at least some of the improvement being on the asymptote. And many writers have explained the superior recall of earliest items in the free-recall list (the primacy effect) as being due to the additional rehearsal, and hence coding, which they received.

The first function of rehearsal, the continued circulation of codings of items in terms of their acoustic-articulatory or specific visual features, might well be incompatible with the active processing specified as its second function. For the continuous recoding in terms of these less deep levels of processing might prevent coding to deeper levels (Jacoby, 1973). This supposes, however, with Morton (1970), that the acoustic-articulatory coding recurs with each rehearsal. It is possible, however, that the recirculation requires so little coding time that it permits deeper coding to occur. It may therefore be conceived of as a strategy employed in cases where a list of unstructured items is presented at a fast rate. It would have the function of maintaining attention on the items to be coded more deeply. The situation could be considered one of divided attention, with the subject using the strategy of recirculation to attend to the previously presented items which he is still coding, and at the same time attending to the currently-being-presented items. Thus the limitation should not be defined in terms of capacity of STS; it is of the rate at which information can be processed thoroughly, i.e. coded deeply.

7.3.2 Rehearsal as coding and strategy

If STS is better considered as an active process rather than a passive store, is it worth distinguishing STS from LTS? The function of rehearsal in recirculating the items coded in a less deep level may be seen as a specific strategy employed in a situation where the rate of input is high. And the function of coding in these experimental situations is no different from that of the many forms of coding which have been reviewed in this book. There are additional difficulties with the notion of information flow from STS to LTS which make this solution increasingly attractive. Firstly, the direction of information flow is seen as being from sensory register via STS to LTS. But the items registered by the senses have to be either selected for attention to be paid to them, or they have to be allowed to fade. Similarly, if items are being coded by well-learned codes in STS, there has to be contact with the LTS structures from which these codes are derived. Alternatively, if the coding devices are conscious strategies, these too presuppose LTS involvement. So also does the strategy of recirculation itself. Thus one does not seem justified in speaking of a one-way flow of information.

Further, there is difficulty with the notion of transfer from one store to another. At what point in the flow diagram does material actually become stored in LTS? Norman (1968) rejects the notion of transfer, and speaks instead of two types of connection of sensorily received material with LTS. First the registered material makes connections with its permanent already existing representation in LTS. However, in addition LTS will scan for certain *expected* features of the stimulus, these expectations being based on contextual coding of the situation. In other words, Norman suggests that before we even start to pay attention to material in order to code it elaboratively we have already selected it (coded it!) in terms of its 'pertinence' or relevance to the situation.

In brief, it appears that one can distinguish a passive view of rehearsal, where it is taken to have the function of recirculating the nominal items, from an active view. In the latter, rehearsal is seen as a process whereby the nominal items are being coded. It seems more parsimonious to deal with this situation by the use of the concepts of coding and of specific strategies. This leaves open the extent to which 'STS' is an inherent structural feature of the system. It might on the contrary be true that we seldom need to recirculate items in the way in which the STM paradigms force us to. For it is seldom that we have to cope with a rapid sequence of verbal material unconnected either within itself or with the situational context. This view also allows recirculation to be a strategy by which one can retain temporarily both nominal items *and* functional units.

If this is so, the strategy of 'recirculation' rehearsal could be considered as an occasional aid for use in artificial situations. Its power should not be underestimated, however; it is a flexible enough tool to not only recirculate and subsequently permit the coding of items which we have to remember, but also to omit material we have been told to forget. This essentially is the import of the findings in the area of 'directed forgetting' (Bjork, 1972; Epstein, 1972), where subjects are told not to remember certain items. This they can do, without the omission interfering in the least with recall of the to-be-remembered items.

7.4 Structure and process

7.4.1 Coding and the serial position effect
If the notions of coding and specific strategy are preferable to the ambiguous catch-all concept of rehearsal, then the whole structuralist picture of the information processing system as a set of stores may likewise be inappropriate. One does need to tie function to structure; the biologists have taught us how important this is. But it is dangerous to infer a structure before we have any real idea how complex function may be. The complexity of human coding processes is only beginning to be discovered; our slowness in discovering them may in part be attributed to the inhibiting effect upon the scope of research which premature structural models have had.

Murdock (1972), however, rightly recalls us to the function of theory and experiment: 'Sooner or later a generally acceptable model of memory and human information processing will emerge, and we should expend every effort to bring it about sooner rather than later' (p. 121). Any theory, whether of a structural or a process orientation, has to deal with the data.

And, as has been demonstrated, the evidence based on the serial position curve must be a major part of any theory. Therefore these results must be accounted for in terms of the levels of coding hypothesis if it is to be considered as a viable alternative to the STS versus LTS distinction.

It is not too hard to describe the primacy and recency results in a general way in terms of coding processes. It will be recalled that variables such as list length, rate of presentation and word frequency had an effect on the asymptote but not on the recency portion of the curve. The numbers of items presented on the interpolated task between presentation and recall affected the recency portion of the curve; so did the grouping of items at presentation, either by temporal groupings or by common word sequences (proverbs). If the divided attention approach to list processing is accepted, then at any given point in the list presentation, the subject is coding earlier items in a deeper way but also registering and coding presently incoming items in a less deep way.

Specifically, he may apply only an acoustic-articulatory coding to the presently incoming information in order to be able to recirculate it for deeper coding later. When the end of the list arrives, the subject has a backlog of circulating items to be coded more deeply. Thus, any demand for recall within five or six seconds of the end of the list may result in some items still being uncoded at a deeper level. Therefore at recall there will be some codings still circulating in an acoustic-articulatory form. The subject may well recall these immediately available items first. This is a reasonable strategy to employ, since the loss of any of the acoustic-articulatory attributes would make retrieval impossible: there are no alternative cues for retrieval. The last few items of a list are *worse* recalled when recall is not immediate (Craik, 1970), implying that the coding of the last few items is very ineffective. Further, the provision of semantic cues at the beginning of the recall period results in worse recall than their provision after subjects have recalled the first rapid group (Loess and Harris, 1968); semantic retrieval cues are of no use if the subject has only coded at an acoustic-articulatory level.

If this account is accurate, then the finding of the imperviousness of the recency effect to sundry variables which *do* effect the asymptote is quite comprehensible. Word frequency should have little effect on acoustic-articulatory coding. Such coding can occur well within a second, so varying the rate of presentation within the usual limits should have no effect. And the length of the list is immaterial if deeper level coding always tags along the same distance behind acoustic-articulatory coding. These variables, on the other hand, *would* be expected to affect deeper level coding; more frequent words should be more rapidly encoded into their semantic attributes; faster rate of presentation should prevent much deeper level coding from occurring; and greater length of list results in greater difficulty of retrieval, with items having to be coded by more attributes to distinguish them from other items. The fact that temporal grouping increases the recency effect could be explained in terms of the ease of recirculation which would result. The ability to filter out repetitions of the same item requires articulatory matching only for identity to be established.

7.4.2 Depth and degree of coding

However, if this were the whole story, we would expect to find that the generalization of acoustic coding in STS and semantic in LTS was largely true. It was noted earlier that there are too many exceptions for this to be the case. It is worth noting what these exceptions are. Firstly, Shulman (1970, 1972) has found that, given a slower rate of presentation, making semantic coding relevant results in successful semantic coding in an STM task. Bruce and Crowley (1970) found that acoustic-articulatory coding was employed in an LTM task when its potential use as a coding device was made very obvious. The other exceptions also show the possibility of more than one form of coding being employed in LTM tasks.

Perhaps a tentative generalization might be as follows. In LTM tasks, subjects can usually code as much as they wish. They will normally employ semantic codes, since these are better for retrieval purposes. However, in STM tasks, subjects can initially (i.e. for circulatory rehearsal) only code by one form of coding. There is no time for further coding. The usual form of coding selected for this task is the acoustic-articulatory form, which lends itself to overt or covert vocalization and takes very little time to apply. However, when encouraged to do so and given the time per item required, subjects can use semantic coding for this purpose. The essential feature of circulatory rehearsal, then, is that it involves the *maintenance* of a simple form of coding of one type or another. Usually, the acoustic-articulatory type is employed because the presentation rate is such that semantic coding is not possible; semantic structure in the material may then actually be a hindrance (Craik and Levy, 1970). The upshot is that the level of coding analogy does not imply an invariable fixed order of coding from less deep, physical, to deeper, semantic forms. Rather, a form of coding may be selected to suit the task situation. Depth of coding, moreover, may be treated in terms of number of different forms of coding employed in a task as well as in terms of the form of coding employed. In general, however, it is true to say that the shorter the time available for processing, the more primitive the coding; the more meaningful the material, the more meaningful the coding; and finally that there is an interaction of speed of coding with meaningfulness of material: the more meaningful the material, the faster the coding processes can occur.

However, it must also be stressed that the very notion of coding language material in a non-meaningful way is almost a contradiction in terms. It is only when we are considering the recall of lists of words, digits or nonsense syllables that the use of non-meaningful attributes for coding will occur. It will be argued in the next section that the coding processes evidenced in the experimental study of verbal memory must be considered in the context of their natural function – communication.

7.5   Memory, language and cognition

7.5.1   The communicative function of language

By now the paradox of memory research cannot have failed to become apparent to the reader. The 'simpler' the material, the more likely the subject is to adopt complex conscious strategies in coding it. All efforts to remove 'confounding' factors of structure and meaning only result in the subject going to great lengths to impose them. This paradox has resulted from the use by the experimenter of verbal material. Verbal material can be coded by any one of the several forms of coding associated with language – phonological, grammatical, semantic. It thus offers interesting alternatives, and leads to the concept of levels of coding appropriate to the task. However, the forms of coding applied by subjects to verbal material normally have a specific function. This function is *not* that of recall in episodic memory tasks, but that of understanding and speaking language. The forms of coding used by subjects in verbal learning and memory tasks do not come from an omni-purpose intellectual tool kit. They come from a very efficient system designed specifically for communication (see 3.1.1).

Consider the communication situation. Typically, the speaker gives utterance with the intention of affecting the behaviour of the listener in some way. He may wish the listener to make a verbal reply. On the other hand, he may wish him to direct his attention to something in the environment, to perform some physical action like closing a door, to cease from some activity, to laugh, to look at the speaker, and so on. Thus the listener has to decode the utterance in such a way as to be able to regulate his behaviour in the desired way (or to refuse to do so). Therefore the function of the utterance is to reduce the listener's uncertainty as to what the desired behaviour is to zero. There will as a result be a lot of redundancy in the signal, and the listener will be able to construct a meaning from multiple cues. Further, this meaning will be a relation of *abstract* attributes, since it has to be used to direct subsequent behaviour often of a non-verbal kind. The main task of the listener, then, is to code in terms of the meaning; any form of coding he uses will be directed to this end. Phonological and grammatical cues are employed not to aid memory but to help to construct an interpretation of the message.

The reverse is true of the speaker. He has to construct a message from a relation of abstract attributes in such a way that the listener will decode the intended meaning and direct his behaviour accordingly. Thus he will use the different forms of linguistic coding required in the situation. Before he can do so, however, he must have the cognitive capacity to form relations between abstract attributes. This has become clear from recent studies of the development of children's language (Slobin, 1972). These show that when the context of the utterance as well as its structure is taken into account, several different semantic relations must have been mastered before certain linguistic structures can be uttered. For example, the utterance 'Mummy shoes' can imply possession, actor and object of action, etc. Thus a certain level of cognitive development is necessary for communicative use of the language system.

This, then, is the system we are tapping when we present

subjects with a verbal episodic memory task. But we are using it for quite different purposes from that for which it was designed. We must expect its normal purpose to be evidenced in the way it is used in this abnormal task. That is, the presentation phase of an episodic memory task may be treated as a listening comprehension task by the subject, the recall phase as a production or utterance task. It is not suggested that the subject consciously adopts this as a strategy, but rather that the forms of coding he uses make it inevitable. The implications are clear: coding at presentation will be in terms of discovering meaning; decoding at recall will be in terms of constructing a message from a meaning. Verbatim recall is atypical, since construction of a message is in terms of effective communication, not perfect reproduction. Verbatim recall may, therefore, differ in that phonological and syntactic codings may also be retained. But meaning is central.

Thus the findings concerning coding of verbal material are not synonymous with findings about memory processes *per se*. Nor do they give grounds for hypothesizing a particular memory structure in terms of STS and LTS. What they *do* show is that we are capable of using linguistic codes in a memorizing task. The fact that different levels of coding ranging from acoustic-articulatory to semantic may be distinguished is a property of the linguistic system rather than a property of memory. The dominance of semantic coding is probably due to the communicative function of language. But the highly complex set of semantic codings developed to express different relations between attributes also happens to be very useful in retrieving items in episodic memory. Therefore its use is appropriate to the task concerned. Moreover, while speakers and listeners have to construct messages from meaning and meaning from messages, memorizers do not *necessarily* have to do so. They may use non-meaningful forms of coding to memorize, indicating that while the communicative function of language has an effect, this effect can be regulated by conscious control strategies.

7.5.2 Communication and memory
The point that the communicative function of language and memory research may be closely connected is well taken by Glanzer (1972), a psychologist who has in fact spent much time in distinguishing STS from LTS. However, he suggests that structural features of the memory system as evidenced by verbal

memory experiments are necessary for linguistic function. In other words, he adopts the reverse logic to that presented in the previous section, arguing from the assumption of STS to its function to aid comprehension and production. I have been arguing that these communicative functions of language have in fact shaped the subject's coding behaviour in the artificial episodic memory task. Therefore much of what has been inferred about episodic memory for linguistic material may be specific to linguistic material.

Glanzer suggests that STS exists as a structural feature of the information processing system because of its part in the comprehension and production of language. Its function in comprehension, he suggests, is to retain words while they are grouped or coded into linguistic units. He conceives of this process as an interpretative one, in which grammatical and lexical knowledge from LTS is applied to the input. The grammatical coding helps to isolate units which may correspond to units in the person's lexicon. Continuous recycling from STS to LTS and vice versa is supposed to occur until an interpretation is registered in LTS. The major point seems to be that STS permits linguistic material to be held in order to be unitized; and it permits the units (e.g. phrases) to be held in order to be interpreted.

This view accords with that presented earlier (6.2.1) to the extent that it sees grammatical coding as an adjunct to semantic coding. However, it does not accord with the idea that subjects code into semantic attributes. By supposing that what is 'in the lexicon' are groups of linguistic units such as words, phrases, and clauses, Glanzer has to infer that coded units are retained verbatim in STS until they can be interpreted as a sequence (i.e. until the whole utterance can be interpreted). And by assuming that material has to be passed through STS to be coded in the first place he has to infer that words have to be rehearsed for this grammatical chunking to occur. Clearly, these two assumptions do result in considerable weight being thrown on active STS; therefore they lend support to Glanzer's suggestion that STS plays a large part in language comprehension.

However, it has been argued earlier that these assumptions are not justified. Subjects rapidly code utterances into semantic attributes; verbatim recall of connected discourse occurs only within the currently-being-uttered sentence (3.2.3). Moreover, they may normally have derived from the context such strong expectations as to what the rest of an utterance is going to be that they only process the first clause to any great depth. Attention to the first clause seems sufficient to remove ambiguity (6.2.2). Thus the picture is not one of a listener painfully building up a sequence of units of language which he can interpret. Rather, he automatically constructs a very rapid hypothesis, in terms of abstract semantic attributes and their relations, of how the utterance is to be interpreted. Then he may check, often desultorily, whether the rest of the utterance does in fact fit this advance construction. Often he may not check at all, being far too busy planning a reply.

Given that communicative function results in coding in terms of meaning, and given that coding for meaning is a rapid construction based on expectations derived from context as well as from past linguistic input, then what implications does this have for the interpretation of the results of memory experiments reviewed in this book? First, it suggests that some types of coding will not be used, not because 'memory' does not use them, but because, from the point of view of communicative function, they are irrelevant. Thus, for example, grammatical form class is an important form of coding for phrases or sentences; but where individual words are presented in a list, it does not function as a coding device to any extent (see 3.1.2, 3.1.3 and 5.1.1). This is because grammatical coding is only relevant where it is an adjunct to discovering meaning — that is, in connected discourse where words can be grouped together to be coded semantically (see 6.2.2). Thus it is suggested that only certain forms of coding are adopted not because of the nature of memory but because of the communicative function of language.

A second implication is that a great deal of our coding of structured material such as discourse or sentences is extremely rapid and automatic (4.1.2). In Posner and Warren's (1972) terms, input taps semantic memory directly. Therefore the role of conscious attention and rehearsal may be considerably smaller than is usually thought. They may be specific strategies for atypical tasks, not structural features in the memory system.

7.5.3 Memory and cognitive development
An important result of the communicative function of language was, it was suggested, the fact that the product of coding was an

abstract meaning. It had to be, since the listener had to use it to regulate subsequent non-linguistic as much as linguistic behaviour. This implies that before a person can use language codes in memory to real advantage, he has to have attained a certain level of cognitive (linguistic?) operations upon abstract attributes of meaning.

There is some evidence that this is so. Research on children suggests that certain forms of organizational coding require operational thinking, and do not occur till 9 or 10 years of age. A review of the developmental literature (Herriot, Green and McConkey, 1973) comes up with the following generalization. Category clustering in free recall may be evidenced in children as young as 3 years, but clustering associated with increased recall does not occur till much later. Clustering on its own can be the result of a sequential form of coding between each item, but clustering associated with increased recall probably requires a coding of a relation. If the analysis in 5.4.3 is correct, subjects need to code items both separately and also in terms of shared attributes. This implies a subsuming of subordinates under a superordinate at storage, and a generation of subordinates from superordinate at retrieval. It requires, in other words, the operations of class inclusion that are a typical feature of operational but not of pre-operational thinking in the child.

A related form of evidence is the experimentation on retarded subjects (Herriot et al., 1973). Subjects of a vocabulary age of 7 or 8 years are unable to organize spontaneously a randomly ordered list of categorical items in a free-recall task. However, given the instruction to remember together the things that belong together, subjects cluster and recall more. Their difficulty was in seeing the appropriateness of the strategy to the task. They could perform the cognitive operations required without further help. Subjects of a vocabulary age of 5 or 6 years, however, only increased their clustering, not their recall.

Other research linking memory performance to cognitive development concerns the STS versus LTS distinction. Thurm and Glanzer (1971) find that 5- and 6-year-olds differ in their asymptote but not in their recency performance. Belmont and Butterfield (1969) discovered that older children spend differential amounts of time coding different items; younger children do not. Their technique was an ingenious one whereby subjects could themselves determine the length of time for which an item was presented. Both these results indicate age-related differences in LTS. Thus the younger children may not have the depth of semantic coding available to them that would enable them to retrieve the bulk of the words adequately. They do, however, have the capability of circulatory rehearsal (supposing this process is evidenced by the recency effect). The same is true of older people — 65-year-old subjects are inferior to 22-year-olds on the asymptote but not on the recency portions of the curve (Craik, 1968) — and of retarded subjects (Ellis, 1970). Finally, there is the evidence that some attributes of meaning are acquired at an earlier age than others (see 3.2.2 and 5.2.3).

One may, perhaps, distinguish two aspects of coding processes which both relate to cognitive development. The first concerns, simply, the depth of coding available at different stages of cognitive development. The results showing inferior performance by younger children on the asymptote suggest that less coding occurred or that less deep coding occurred. The evidence that younger children categorize material more in terms of its physical than its functional features favours the latter alternative. The second aspect of memory coding processes related to cognitive development concerns the complexity of the operations performed upon the coded attributes. Certain operations seem to be dependent upon the attainment of operational thinking.

7.6 The status of memory research

7.6.1 The present
We are left with what appear at first sight to be some rather gloomy conclusions. Most memory research has consisted of episodic memory for verbal material. Therefore the coding processes which have been evidenced are likely to be accidental by-products of the communicative function of language or consciously developed strategies to cope with the task. Language function in its turn appears to depend upon a certain level of cognitive development, the ability to perform certain sorts of operation upon abstract semantic attributes. There seem to be other, more effective, ways of investigating the understanding and production of language and the cognitive functioning of the individual than by giving him episodic memory tasks.

On the other hand, it might be argued that we are not only interested in discovering the linguistic and cognitive processes of the individual in those situations for which they were specifically developed. We may not, for example, be concerned only with language as a means of communication. Rather, we may be interested in discovering how individuals employ these well-formed and practised processes when faced with a novel task. We are not so much concerned that episodic memory findings might not be generalizable; we are, on the contrary, pleased to discover that linguistic processes are.

However, care must be taken in the sort of inferences which are drawn from this body of research. We cannot infer that memory processes can be identified with certain specific forms of coding. For example, we cannot conclude that in memory tasks the basic form of coding is semantic. This is generalizing in an unjustifiable way from episodic memory for verbal material. What we can do is to indicate the potential flexibility and variety of the way a human being *can* deal with his experience. What we have demonstrated, in other words, is competence. Thus it is a good thing that we have employed verbal material, since its use has resulted in the subject having the amazingly flexible tool of language at his disposal. If most memory research had employed visual material, we might not have appreciated the ways in which we can adapt our well-learned processes to new tasks.

We are dealing, then, with coding processes which subjects use in memory tasks; we do not identify specific *forms* of coding as memory processes, since their use is a product of the particular material chosen by the experimenter. We can, however, speak of the *capabilities* of the human being as a processor of information. Because subjects have shown themselves capable of flexible strategies and varied forms of coding in the case of verbal material, then we know that we cannot fix any arbitrary limit on their abilities which is lower than that evidenced in verbal memory tasks. We cannot, of course, fix limits at all; but at least the memory task has at last forced us to consider the human organism as a creative actor upon his environment.

It may be worthwhile to specify the generalizations (based on memory research) which can be made about the capabilities of the human organism. First, he can code and transform the material presented: there must be a distinction between the nominal and the functional stimulus. Second, this coding can be into attributes, which he can abstract and then operate upon. Third, these operations may be highly predictable and practised, or they may be novel, the result of conscious strategies for task solution. Finally, he can become aware of the fact that he has these capabilities.

7.6.2 The future
Where does memory research go in the future?

Since an experiment into memory does not need to be an episodic memory experiment, then we may expect to find many more experiments into the perception and comprehension of verbal and other material, and also into retrieval from semantic memory. The need to distinguish automatic from conscious processing will result in more careful selection of tasks. Tasks aimed at revealing automatic processing will involve the subject in meaningful processing of meaningful material within a meaningful context. Tasks aimed at revealing conscious processing will be selected with that objective in mind; they will not be hangovers from outmoded conceptions of human function. Rather, they will permit the subject selection of alternative strategies and take note of his reports on what strategy he has used. Alternatively, the experimenter may instruct the subject which strategy to use (Reitman, 1970), with a view to discovering each strategy's effectiveness.

The concept of levels of coding will receive much wider attention. It will be a matter for debate and empirical resolution whether the order from less deep to deeper coding is always followed, or whether improved performance results as much from number of forms of coding employed as from the depth of coding reached. Further, the notion of depth will be refined as we learn more about attributes. The specification of some of the underlying semantic attributes will result in their use for coding purposes being explored. We should come to learn how different levels of semantic coding are employed in storage and retrieval. And our findings will be based on subjects' own attributes, not on cues intuited by the experimenter.

Moreover, we will learn more about the actual operations or processes which the subject employs when coding or reconstructing. It will become evident that memory processes, cognitive processes and linguistic processes can only be distinguished on the basis of the experimental task, not on the basis of their intrinsic differences.

Model-makers will continue to approximate more and more closely by their mathematical skill to an adequate account of certain experiments, granted certain assumptions: but their assumptions will be more closely questioned and their limitations of the corpus of experiments which they can account for by their models will be challenged. On the other hand, the decreasing emphasis on structural constraints and the sequential processing of information will enable them to employ mathematical techniques of greater abstractness and power (Broadbent, 1971; Murdock, 1972). The use of computer programmes to model memory processes will also flourish. But both computer and mathematical modellers will have to write alternative programmes or formulae in such a way that it is possible to test experimentally which is the better model; for several alternatives may adequately describe the results as they stand at present.

Finally, the emphasis will change from structure to process, from limitations to capabilities, and from separate areas of research to a common view of man as an active coder of his environment. Memory research is potentially the unifying force by which experimental psychology can be persuaded to adopt these changes in emphasis. We have only just begun.

Appendix

The following is a list of books partly or wholly devoted to memory. They are in approximate order of difficulty.

HUNTER, I. M. (1964). *Memory*. Harmondsworth, Penguin.
CERMAK, L. S. (1972). *Human Memory: Research and Theory*. New York, Ronald.
NORMAN, D. A. (1969). *Memory and Attention*. New York, Wiley.
ADAMS, J. (1967). *Human Memory*. New York, McGraw-Hill.
DODWELL, P. C. (Ed.) (1972). *New Horizons in Psychology*, Vol. II. Harmondsworth, Penguin.
KINTSCH, W. (1970). *Learning, Memory and Conceptual Processes*. New York, Wiley.
SUMMERFIELD, A. (Ed.) (1971). *Cognitive Psychology. British Medical Bulletin*, Vol. 27, 3.
DIXON, T. R. and HORTON, D. L. (Eds.) (1968). *Verbal Behavior and General Behavior Theory*. Englewood Cliffs, Prentice-Hall.
MELTON, A. W. and MARTIN, E. (Eds.) (1972). *Coding Processes in Human Memory*. New York, Winston.
TULVING, E. and DONALDSON, W. A. (Eds.) (1972). *Organisation of Memory*. New York, Academic Press.
NORMAN, D. A. (ed.) (1970). *Models of Human Memory*. New York, Academic Press.

A book of readings is
POSTMAN, L. and KEPPEL, G. (Eds.) (1971). *Verbal Learning and Memory*. Harmondsworth, Penguin.

Volumes which form an at present unfinished series are

BOWER, G. H. (Ed.). *The Psychology of Learning and Motivation.* Early volumes were edited by K. W. and J. T. Spence, more recent volumes by J. T. Spence and Bower or by Bower alone; thus far six volumes, spanning 1966-72. New York, Academic Press.

See also the *Annual Review of Psychology.*

Journals most likely to contain relevant research are:

Journal of Verbal Learning and Verbal Behavior
Journal of Experimental Psychology
Memory and Cognition
Cognitive Psychology
Psychological Review
Psychological Bulletin

Bibliography

Abbreviations: *JVLVB = Journal of Verbal Learning and Verbal Behavior*
JEP = Journal of Experimental Psychology

ADAMS, J. A. and McINTYRE, J. S. (1967). Natural language mediation and all-or-none learning. *Canadian Journal of Psychology*, 21, 36—49.

ADAMS, J. A. and MONTAGUE, W. E. (1967). Retroactive inhibition and natural language mediation. *JVLVB*, 6, 528—35.

ANDERSON, J. R. and BOWER, G. H. (1972). Recognition and retrieval processes in free recall. *Psychological Review*, 79, 97—123.

ANISFELD, M. and KNAPP, M. (1968). Association, synonymy, and directionality and false recognition. *JEP*, 77 171—9.

ATKINSON, R. C. and JUOLA, J. F. (1973). Factors influencing speed and accuracy of word recognition. In Kornblum, S. (Ed.). *Attention and Performance*, Vol. IV. New York, Academic Press.

ATKINSON, R. C. and SHIFFRIN, R. M. (1968). Human memory: a proposed system and its control processes. In Spence, K. W. and Spence, J. T. (Eds.). *The Psychology of Learning and Motivation*, Vol. 2. New York, Academic Press.

BACHARACH, V. R. and KELLAS, G. (1971). Phrase versus base structure effects on short-term retention. *JVLVB*, 10, 171—5.

BADDELEY, A. D. (1968). How does acoustic similarity influence short-term memory? *Quarterly Journal of Experimental Psychology*, 20, 249—64.

BADDELEY, A. D. (1972a). Human memory. In Dodwell, P. C. (Ed.). *New Horizons in Psychology*, Vol. II. Harmondsworth, Penguin.

BADDELEY, A. D. (1972b). Retrieval rules and semantic coding in short-term memory. *Psychological Bulletin*, 78, 379—85.

BADDELEY, A. D. and PATTERSON, K. (1971). The relation between long-term and short-term memory. *British Medical Bulletin*, **27**, 237—42.

BADDELEY, A. D. and WARRINGTON, E. K. (1970). Amnesia and the distinction between long- and short-term memory. *JVLVB*, **9**, 176—89.

BAHRICK, H. P. (1969). Measurement of memory by prompted recall. *JEP*, **79**, 213—19.

BARTLETT, F. C. (1932). *Remembering*. Cambridge, Cambridge University Press.

BATTIG, W. F. and MONTAGUE, W. E. (1969). Category norms for verbal items in 56 categories: a replication and extension of the Connecticut Category Norms. *Journal of Experimental Psychology Monograph*, **80**, 1—46.

BEGG, I. and PAIVIO, A. (1969). Concreteness and imagery in sentence meaning. *JVLVB*, **8**, 821—7.

BELMONT, J. M. and BUTTERFIELD, E. C. (1969). The relations of short-term memory to development and intelligence. In Lipsitt, L. P. and Reese, H. W. (Eds.). *Advances in Child Development |Behavior*, Vol. 4. New York, Academic Press.

BEVAN, W., DUKES, W. F. and AVANT, L. (1966). The effect of variation in specific stimuli on memory for their superordinates. *American Journal of Psychology*, **79**, 250—7.

BEVER, T. G., GARRETT, M. F. and HURTIG, R. (1973). The interaction of perceptual processes and ambiguous sentences. *Memory and Cognition*, **1**, 277—86.

BJORK, R. A. (1970). Repetition and rehearsal mechanisms in models for short-term memory. In Norman, D. A. (Ed.). *Models of Human Memory*. New York, Academic Press.

BJORK, R. A. (1972). Theoretical implications of directed forgetting. In Melton, A. W. and Martin, E. (Eds.). *Coding Processes in Human Memory*. Washington D.C., Winston.

BLAKE, M. (1973). Prediction of recognition when recall fails: explaining the feeling of knowing phenomenon. *JVLVB*, **12**, 311—19.

BOBROW, S. A. and BOWER, G. H. (1969). Comprehension and recall of sentences. *JEP*, **80**, 55—61.

BOUSFIELD, W. A. (1953). The occurrence of clustering in recall of randomly arranged associates. *Journal of General Psychology*, **49**, 269—73.

BOUSFIELD, W. A., PUFF, C. R. and COWAN, T. M. (1964). The development of constancies in sequential organisation during repeated free recall. *JVLVB*, **3**, 489—95.

BOUSFIELD, A. K. and BOUSFIELD, W. A. (1966). Measurement of clustering and of sequential constancies in repeated free recall. *Psychological Reports*, **19**, 935—42.

BOWER, G. H. (1970a). Mental imagery and associative learning. In Gregg, L. (Ed.). *Cognition in Learning and Memory*. New York, Wiley.

BOWER, G. H. (1970b). Organisational factors in memory. *Cognitive Psychology*, **1**, 18—46.

BOWER, G. H. (1972a). Stimulus-sampling theory of encoding variability. In Melton, A. W. and Martin, E. (Eds.) *Coding Processes in Human Memory.* Washington D.C., Winston.

BOWER, G. H. (1972b). A selective review of organisational factors in memory. In Tulving E. and Donaldson, W. A. (Eds.) *Organization of Memory.* New York, Academic Press.

BOWER, G. H., CLARK, M. C., LESGOLD, A. M. and WINZENZ, D. (1969) Hierarchical retrieval schemes in recall of categorised word lists. *JVLVB*, 8, 323–43.

BOWER, G. H. and REITMAN, J. S. (1972). Mnemonic elaboration in multilist learning. *JVLVB*, 11, 478–85.

BRANSFORD, J. D. and FRANKS, J. J. (1971). The abstraction of linguistic ideas. *Cognitive Psychology*, 2, 331–50.

BREGMAN, A. S. and STRASBERG, R. (1968). Memory for the syntactic form of sentences. *JVLVB*, 7, 396–403.

BROADBENT, D. E. (1958). *Perception and Communication.* London, Pergamon.

BROADBENT, D. E. (1971). *Decision and Stress.* New York, Academic Press.

BROWN, J. (1958). Some tests of the decay theory of immediate memory. *Quarterly Journal of Experimental Psychology*, 10, 12–21.

BROWN, R. W. and McNEILL, D. (1966). The tip of the tongue phenomenon. *JVLVB*, 5, 325–37.

BRUCE, D. and CROWLEY, J. J. (1970). Acoustic similarity effects on retrieval from secondary memory. *JVLVB*, 9, 190–6.

BRUCE, D. and MURDOCK, B. B. Jun. (1968). Acoustic similarity effects on memory for paired associates. *JVLVB*, 7, 627–31.

BRUCE, D. J. (1958). The effect of listener's anticipation on the intelligibility of heard speech. *Language and Speech*, 1, 79–97.

BUTLER, B. E. and MERIKLE, P. M. (1970). Uncertainty and meaningfulness in paired-associate learning. *JVLVB*, 9, 634–41.

CARROLL, J. B. and WHITE, M. N. (1973). Word frequency and age of acquisition as determiners of picture-naming latency. *Quarterly Journal of Experimental Psychology*, 25, 85–95.

CERMAK, L. S. (1972). *Human Memory: Research and Theory.* New York, Ronald.

CHAPIN, P. G., SMITH, T. S. and ABRAHAMSON, A. A. (1972). Two factors in perceptual segmentation of speech. *JVLVB*, 11, 164–73.

CHOMSKY, N. (1957). *Syntactic Structures.* The Hague, Mouton.

CHOMSKY, N. (1965). *Aspects of the theory of syntax.* Cambridge, Mass., M.I.T. Press.

CLARK, H. H. and CHASE, W. G. (1972). On the process of comparing sentences against pictures. *Cognitive Psychology*, 3, 472–517.

COFER, C. N. (1966). Some evidence for coding processes derived from clustering in free recall. *JVLVB*, 5, 188–97.

COFER, C. N. (1967). Does conceptual organization influence the amount retained in immediate free recall? In Kleinmuntz, B. (Ed.) *Concepts and the Structure of Memory.* New York, Wiley.

COFER, C. N. and BRUCE, D. R. (1965). Form-class as the basis for clustering in the recall of non-associated words. *JVLVB*, 4, 386—9.

COHEN, B. H. (1966). Some-or-none characteristics of coding behaviour. *JVLVB*, 5, 182—7.

COLLE, H. A. (1972). The reification of clustering. *JVLVB*, 11, 624—33.

COLLINS, A. M. and QUILLIAN, M R. (1969). Retrieval time from semantic memory. *JVLVB*, 8, 240—7.

COLLINS, A. M. and QUILLIAN, M. R. (1970). Does category size affect categorization time? *JVLVB*, 9, 432-8.

COLLINS, A. M. and QUILLIAN, M. R. (1972). How to make a language user. In Tulving, E. and Donaldson, W. A. (Eds.) *Organization of Memory*. New York, Academic Press.

COLTHEART, M. (1972). Visual information-processing. In Dodwell, P. C. (Ed.) *New Horizons in Psychology*, Vol. II. Harmondsworth, Penguin.

CONRAD, C. (1972). Cognitive economy in semantic memory. *JEP*, 92, 149—54.

CONRAD, R. (1964). Acoustic confusions in immediate memory. *British Journal of Psychology*, 55, 75—84.

CONRAD, R. and HULL, A. J. (1964). Information, acoustic confusion, and memory span. *British Journal of Psychology*, 55, 429—32.

CONRAD, R. and HULL, A. J. (1968). Input modality and the serial position curve in short-term memory. *Psychonomic Science*, 10, 135—6.

CRAIK, F. I. M. (1968). Two components in free recall. *JVLVB*, 7, 996—1004.

CRAIK, F. I. M. (1969). Modality effects in free recall. *JVLVB*, 8, 665-76.

CRAIK, F. I. M. (1970). The fate of primary memory items in free recall. *JVLVB*, 9, 143—8.

CRAIK, F. I. M. (1971). Primary memory. *British Medical Bulletin*, 27, 232—6.

CRAIK, F. I. M. (1973). A 'levels of analysis' view of memory. To appear in Kliner, P., Krames, L. and Alloway, T. M. (Eds.) *Communication and Affect, Language, and Thought*. New York, Academic Press (in press).

CRAIK, F. I. M. and LEVY, B. A. (1970). Semantic and acoustic information in primary memory. *JEP*, 86, 77—82.

CRAIK, F. I. M. and LOCKHART, R. S. (1972). Levels of processing: a framework for memory research. *JVLVB*, 11, 671—84.

CRAMER, P. (1970). Semantic generalisation: IAR locus and instructions. *JEP*, 83, 266—73.

CROWDER, R. G. and MORTON, J. (1960). Precategorical acoustic storage (PAS). *Perception and Psychophysics*, 5, 365—73.

DANKS, J. H. and SORCE, P. A. (1973). Imagery and deep structure in the prompted recall of passive sentences. *JVLVB*, 12, 114—17.

DARWIN, C. J., TURVEY, M. T. and CROWDER, R. G. (1972). An auditory analogue of the Sperling partial report procedure: evidence for brief auditory storage. *Cognitive Psychology*, 3, 255—67.

DEESE, J. (1959). Influence of inter-item associative strength upon immediate free recall. *Psychological Reports*, 5, 305—12.

DEESE, J. (1962). On the structure of associative meaning. *Psychological Review*, 69, 166—75.

DEESE, J. (1966). *The Structure of Associations in Language and Thought.* Baltimore, Johns Hopkins Press.

DEESE, J. (1970). *Psycholinguistics.* Boston, Allyn and Bacon.

DE GROOT, A. D. (1965). *Thought and Choice in Chess.* The Hague, Mouton.

DI VESTA, F. J., INGERSOLL, G. and SUNSHINE, P. (1971). A factor analysis of imagery tests. *JVLVB*, 10, 471—9.

DONG, T. and KINTSCH, W. (1968). Subjective retrieval cues in free recall. *JVLVB*, 7, 813—16.

DOOLING, D. J. and LACHMAN, R. (1971). Effect of comprehension on retention of prose. *JEP*, 88, 216—22.

EAGLE, M. N. and ORTOF, E. (1967). The effect of level of attention upon 'phonetic' recognition errors. *JVLVB*, 6, 226—31.

ELIAS, C. S. and PERFETTI, C. A. (1973). Encoding task and recognition memory: the importance of semantic encoding. *JEP*, 99, 151—6.

ELLIS, N. R. (1970). Memory processes in retardates and normals: theoretical and empirical considerations. In Ellis, N. R. (Ed.) *International Review of Research in Mental Retardation*, Vol. 4. New York, Academic Press.

EPSTEIN, W. A. (1961). The influence of syntactical structure on learning. *American Journal of Psychology*, 74, 80—5.

EPSTEIN, W. A. (1972). Mechanisms of directed forgetting. In Bower, G. H. (Ed.).*The Psychology of Learning and Motivation*, Vol. 6. New York, Academic Press.

ESTES, W. K. (1972). An associative basis for coding and organization in memory.In Melton, A. W. and Martin, E. (Ed.) *Coding Processes in Human Memory.* Washington D.C., Winston.

FILLENBAUM, S. and RAPOPORT, A. (1971). *Structures in the Subjective Lexicon.* New York, Academic Press.

FRANKS, J. J. and BRANSFORD, J. D. (1972). The acquisition of abstract ideas. *JVLVB*, 11, 311—15.

FREEDMAN, J. L. and LOFTUS, E. F. (1971). Retrieval of words from long-term memory. *JVLVB*, 10, 107—15.

FROST, N. A. H. (1971). Clustering by visual shape in the free recall of pictorial stimuli. *JEP*, 88, 409—13.

GARDINER, J. M. (1974). Levels of processing in word recognition and subsequent free recall. *JEP* (in press).

GARDINER, J. M., CRAIK, F. I. M. and BLEASDALE, F. A. (1973). Retrieval difficulty and subsequent recall. *Memory and Cognition*, 1, 213—16.

GLANZER, M. (1972). Storage mechanisms in recall. In Bower, G. H.(Ed.) *The Psychology of Learning and Motivation*, Vol. 5. New York, Academic Press.

GLANZER, M. and CUNITZ, A. R. (1966). Two storage mechanisms in free recall. *JVLVB*, 5, 351—60.

GLANZER, M., GIANUTSOS, R. and DUBIN, S. (1969). The removal of items from short-term storage. *JVLVB*, 8, 435—47.

GLANZER, M., KOPPENAAL, L. and NELSON, R. (1972). Effects of relations between words on short-term storage and long-term storage. *JVLVB*, 11, 403—16.

GLANZER, M. and MEINZER, A. (1967). The effects of intra-list activity on free recall. *JVLVB*, 6, 928—35.

GLANZER, M. and SCHWARTZ, A. (1971). Mnemonic structure in free recall: differential effects on STS and LTS. *JVLVB*, 10, 194—8.

GOLDFARB, C. WIRTZ, J. and ANISFELD, M. (1973). Abstract and concrete phrases in false recognition. *JEP*, 98, 25—30.

GOLDMAN-EISLER, F. (1968). *Psycholinguistics: Experiments in Spontaneous Speech.* London, Academic Press.

GREENE, J. (1972). *Psycholinguistics.* Harmondsworth, Penguin.

GRONINGER, L. D. (1966). Natural language mediation and covert rehearsal in short-term memory. *Psychonomic Science,* 5, 135—6.

GUMENIK, W. E. (1969). The effects of articulatory activity and auditory, visual, and semantic similarity on the short-term memory of visually presented paired associates. *JEP*, 82, 70—4.

HART, J. (1967). Memory and the memory-monitoring process. *JVLVB*, 6, 685—91.

HEISEY, J. A. and DUNCAN, C. P. (1971). Syntactical encoding in short-term memory. *JVLVB*, 10, 95—100.

HENRY, N. and VOSS, J. F. (1970). Associative strength growth produced via category membership. *JEP*, 83, 136—40.

HERRIOT, P. (1969). The comprehension of active and passive sentences as a function of pragmatic expectations. *JVLVB*, 8, 166—9.

HERRIOT, P. (1970). *An Introduction to the Psychology of Language.* London, Methuen.

HERRIOT, P., GREEN, J. M. and McCONKEY, R. (1973). *Organisation and Memory: A Review, and a Project in Subnormality.* London, Methuen.

HICKS, R. E. and YOUNG, R. K. (1972). Part-whole list transfer in free recall: a reappraisal. *JEP*, 96, 328—33.

HINRICHS, J. B. (1970). A two-process memory strength theory for judgement of recency. *Psychological Review,* 77, 223—33.

HINTZMAN, D. L. (1967). Articulatory coding in short-term memory. *JVLVB*, 6, 312—16.

HINTZMAN, D. L. (1970). Effects of repetition and exposure duration on memory. *JEP*, 83, 435—44.

HINTZMAN, D. L. and BLOCK, R. A. (1970). Memory judgements and the effect of spacing. *JVLVB*, 9, 561—5.

HINTZMAN, D. L. and BLOCK, R. A. (1971). Repetition and memory: evidence for a multiple-trace hypothesis. *JEP*, 88, 297—306.

HINTZMAN, D. L., BLOCK, R. A. and INSKEEP, N. R. (1972). Memory for mode of input. *JVLVB*, 11, 741—9.

HINTZMAN, D. L. and SUMMERS, J. F. (1973). Long-term visual traces of visually presented words. *Bulletin of the Psychonomic Society,* 1, 325—7.

HOROWITZ, L. M. and MANELIS, L. (1972). Toward a theory of re-integrative memory in adjective-noun phrases. In Bower, G. H. (Ed.) *The Psychology of Learning and Motivation*, Vol. 6. New York, Academic Press.

HOWE, M. J. A. (1970). Repeated presentation and recall of meaningful prose. *Journal of Educational Psychology*, 61, 214—19.

HYDE, T. S. (1973). Differential effects of effort and type of orienting task on recall and organisation of higly associated words. *JEP*, 79, 111—13.

HYDE, T. S. and JENKINS, J. J. (1969). Differential effects of incidental tasks on the organisation of recall of a list of higly associated words. *JEP*, 82, 472—81.

HYDE, T. S. and JENKINS, J. J. (1973). Recall for words as a function of semantic, graphic, and syntactic orienting tasks. *JVLVB*, 12, 471-80.

JACOBY, L. L. (1973). Encoding processes, rehearsal, and recall requirements. *JVLVB*, 12, 302—10.

JAHNKE, J. C. (1968a). Delayed recall and the serial-position effect of short-term memory. *JEP*, 76, 618—22.

JAHNKE, J. C. (1968b). Presentation rate and the serial position effect of immediate serial recall. *JVLVB*, 7, 608—12.

JAKOBSON, R. and HALLE, M. (1956). *Fundamentals of Language*. The Hague, Mouton.

JARVELLA, R. J. (1971). Syntactic processing of connected speech. *JVLVB*, 10, 409—416.

JENKINS, J. B. and DALLENBACH, K. M. (1924). Obliviscence during sleep and waking. *American Journal of Psychology*, 35, 605—12.

JOHNSON, M. G. (1970). A cognitive feature model of compound free-associations. *Psychological Review*, 77, 282—93.

JOHNSON, M. K., BRANSFORD, J. D. and SOLOMON, S. (1973). Memory for tacit implications of sentences. *JEP*, 98, 203—5.

JOHNSON, M. K., BRANSFORD, J. D., NYBERG, S. E. and CLEARY, J. J. (1972). Comprehension factors in interpreting memory for abstract and concrete sentences. *JVLVB*, 11, 451—4.

JOHNSON, N. F. (1968). Sequential verbal behavior. In Dixon, T. R. and Horton, D. L. (Eds.) *Verbal Behavior and General Behavior Theory*. Englewood Cliffs, N. J., Prentice-Hall.

JOHNSON, N. F. (1970). The role of chunking and organization in the process of recall. In Bower, G. H. (Ed.) *The Psychology of Learning and Motivation*, Vol. 4. New York, Academic Press.

JOHNSON, N. F. (1972). Organization and the concept of a memory code. In Melton, A. W. and Martin, E. (Eds.) *Coding Processes in Human Memory*. Washington, D.C., Winston.

JOHNSON-LAIRD, P. N. (1974). Experimental Psycholinguistics. *Annual Review of Psychology*, 25, (in press).

JOHNSTON, C. D. and JENKINS, J. J. (1971). Two more incidental tasks that differentially affect associative clustering in recall. *JEP*, 88, 92—5.

KENDLER, H. H. and WARD, J. W. (1972). Recognition and recall of related and unrelated words. *Psychonomic Science*, 28, 193—5.

KEPPEL, G. and UNDERWOOD, B. J. (1962). Proactive inhibition in short-term retention of single items. *JVLVB*, 1, 153—61.

KIMBLE, G. A. (1968). Mediating associations. *JEP*, 76, 263—6.

KINTSCH, W. (1970a). *Learning, Memory, and Conceptual Processes*. New York, Wiley.

KINTSCH, W. (1970b). Models for free recall and recognition. In Norman, D. A. (Ed.). *Models of Human Memory*. New York, Academic Press.

KINTSCH, W. (1972). Notes on the structure of semantic memory. In Tulving, E. and Donaldson, W. (Eds.). *Organization of Memory*. New York, Academic Press.

KINTSCH, W. and BUSCHKE, H. (1969). Homophones and synonyms in short-term memory. *JEP*, 80, 403—7.

KROLL, N. E. A., PARKS, T., PARKINSON, S. R., BIEBER, S. L. and JOHNSON, A. L. (1970). Short-term memory while shadowing: recall of visually and aurally presented letters. *JEP*, 85, 220—4.

KRUEGER, L. E. (1972). Sentence-picture comparison: a test of additivity of processing time for feature-matching and negation-coding stages. *JEPP*, 95, 275—84.

KUHN, T. S. (1962). *The Structure of Scientific Revolutions*. Chicago, University of Chicago Press.

LACKNER, J. and GARRETT, M. F. (1973). Resolving ambiguity: effects of biasing information in the unattended ear. *Cognition*, (in press).

LANDAUER, T. K. and FREEDMAN, J. L. (1968). Information retrieval from long-term memory: category size and recognition time. *JVLVB*, 7, 291—5.

LANDAUER, T. K. and MEYER, D. E. (1972). Category size and semantic memory retrieval. *JVLVB*, 11, 539—49.

LAUGHERY, K. R. (1969). Computer simulation of short-term memory: a component-decay model. In Spence, J. T. and Bower, G. H. (Eds.). *The Psychology of Learning and Motivation*, Vol. 3. New York, Academic Press.

LESGOLD, A. M. (1972). Pronominalisation: a device for unifying sentences in memory. *JVLVB*, 11, 316—23.

LEVY, B. A. (1971). Role of articulation in auditory and visual short-term memory. *JVLVB*, 10, 123—32.

LEVY, B. A. and MURDOCK, B. B. (JUN.) (1968). The effects of delayed auditory feedback and intralist similarity in short-term memory. *JVLVB*, 7, 887—94.

LIBERMAN, A. M., MATTINGLY, I. G. and TURVEY, M. T. (1972). Language codes and memory codes. In Melton, A. W. and Martin, E. (Eds.). *Coding Processes in Human Memory*. Washington, D.C., Winston.

LIGHT, L. and CARTER—SOBELL, L. (1970). Effects of changed semantic context on recognition memory. *JVLVB*, 9, 1—11.

LINDLEY, R. H. (1965). Effects of trigram-recoding cue complexity on short-term memory. *JVLVB*, 4, 274—9.

LOESS, H. and HARRIS, R. (1968). Short-term memory for individual verbal items as a function of method of recall. *JEP*, 78, 64—9.

LOFTUS, E. F., FREEDMAN, J. L. and LOFTUS, G. R. (1970). Retrieval of words from subordinate and supraordinate categories in semantic hierarchies. *Psychonomic Science*, 21, 235—6.

LOFTUS, E. F. and FREEDMAN, J. L. (1972). Effect of category-name frequency on the speed of naming of an instance of the category. *JVLVB*, 11, 343—7.

LYONS, J. (1968). *Introduction to Theoretical Linguistics*. Cambridge, Cambridge University Press.

LYONS, J. and WALES, R. J. (Eds.) (1971). *New Horizons in Linguistics*. Harmondsworth, Penguin.

MADIGAN, S. A. (1969). Intraserial repetition and coding processes in free recall. *JVLVB*, 8, 828—35.

MADIGAN, S. A. (1971). Modality and recall order interactions in short-term memory for serial order. *JEP*, 87, 294—6.

MALTZMAN, I. (1968). Theoretical conceptions of semantic conditioning and generalisation. In Dixon, T. R. and Horton, D. L. (Eds.) *Verbal Behavior and General Behavior Theory*. Englewood-Cliffs, N. J., Prentice-Hall.

MANDLER, G. (1967). Organisation and memory. In Spence, K. W. and Spence, J. T. (Eds.) *The Psychology of Learning and Motivation*, Vol. 1. New York, Academic Press.

MANDLER, G. (1969). Input variables and output strategies in free recall of categorized words. *American Journal of Psychology*, 82, 531—9.

MANDLER, G. (1972). Organization and recognition. In Tulving, E. and Donaldson, W. A. (Eds.). *Organization of Memory*. New York, Academic Press.

MANDLER, G., and DEAN, P. J. (1969). Seriation: development of serial order in free recall. *JEP*, 81, 207—15.

MANDLER, G. and PEARLSTONE, Z. (1966). Free and constrained concept learning and subsequent recall. *JVLVB*, 5, 126—31.

MARTIN, E. (1968). Stimulus meaningfulness and paired-associate transfer: an encoding variability hypothesis. *Psychological Review*, 75, 421—41.

MARTIN, E. (1970). Toward an analysis of subjective phrase structure. *Psychological Bulletin*, 74, 153—66.

MARTIN, E. (1972). Stimulus encoding in learning and transfer. In Melton, A. W. and Martin, E. (Eds.) *Coding Processes in Human Memory*. Washington, D.C., Winston.

MARTIN, E. and ROBERTS, K. (1966). Grammatical factors in sentence retention. *JVLVB*, 5, 211—18.

MARTIN, J. E., KOLODZIEJ, B. and GENAY, J. (1971). Segmentation of sentences into phonological phrases as a function of constituent length. *JVLVB*, 10, 226—33.

MASSARO, D. W. (1970a). Preperceptual auditory images. *JEP*, 85, 411—17.

MASSARO, D. W. (1970). Perceptual processes and forgetting in memory tasks. *Psychological Review*, 1970, 557—67.

McLEOD, P. D., WILLIAMS, C. E. and BROADBENT, D. E. (1971). Free recall with assistance from one and from two retrieval cues. *British Journal of Psychology*, 62, 59–65.

MEHLER, J. (1963). Some effects of grammatical transformations on the recall of English sentences. *JVLVB*, 2, 246–351.

MELTON, A. W. (1963). Implications of short-term memory for a general theory of memory. *JVLVB*, 2, 1–21.

MELTON, A. W. (1970). The situation with respect to the spacing of repetitions and memory. *JVLVB*, 9, 596–606.

MEYER, D. E. (1970). On the representation and retrieval of stored semantic information. *Cognitive Psychology*, 1, 242–300.

MEYER, D. E. (1973). Correlated operations in searching stored semantic categories. *JEP*, 99, 124–33.

MEYER, D. E. and SCHVANEVELDT, R. W. (1971). Facilitation in recognising pairs of words: evidence of a dependence between retrieval operations. *JEP*, 90, 227–34.

MILLER, G. A. (1956). The magical number seven, plus or minus two: some limits on our capacity for processing information. *Psychological Review*, 63, 81–97.

MILLER, G. A. (1972). English verbs of motion: a case study in semantics and lexical memory. In Melton, A.|W. and Martin, E. (Eds.) *Coding Processes in Human Memory*. Washington, D.C., Winston.

MONTAGUE, W. E., ADAMS, J. A. and KIESS, H. O. (1966). Forgetting and natural language mediation. *JEP*, 72, 829–33.

MORIN, R. E., DE ROSA, D. V. and STULTZ, V. (1967). Recognition memory and reaction time. *Acta Psychologica*, 27, 298–305.

MORTON, J. (1968). Repeated items and decay in memory. *Psychonomic Science*, 10, 219–20.

MORTON, J. (1970). A functional model for memory. In Norman, D. A. (Ed.) *Models of Human Memory*. New York, Academic Press.

MORTON, J. and HOLLOWAY, C. M. (1970). Absence of a cross-modal suffix effect in short-term memory. *Quarterly Journal of Experimental Psychology*, 22, 167–76.

MORTON, J., CROWDER, R. G. and PRUSSIN, H. A. (1971). Experiments with the stimulus suffix effect. *JEP*, 91, 169–90.

MURDOCK, B. B. (JUN.) (1962). The serial position effect of free recall. *JEP*, 64, 482–8.

MURDOCK, B. B. (JUN.) (1963). Short-term memory and paired associate learning. *JVLVB*, 2, 320–8.

MURDOCK, B. B. (JUN.) (1965). Efects of a subsidiary task on short-term memory. *British Journal of Psychology*, 56, 413–19.

MURDOCK, B. B. (JUN.) (1967). Auditory and visual stores in short-term memory. *Acta Psychologica*, 27, 316–24.

MURDOCK, B. B. (JUN.) (1968). Modality effects in short-term memory: storage or retrieval? *JEP*, 77, 79–86.

MURDOCK, B. B. (JUN.) (1972). Short-term memory. In Bower, G. H. (Ed.) *The Psychology of Learning and Motivation*, Vol. 5. New York, Academic Press.

MURDOCK, B. B. (JUN.) and WALKER, K. D. (1969). Modality effects in free recall. *JVLVB*, 8, 665–76.

MURRAY, D. J. (1965). The effect of white noise upon the recall of vocalised lists. *Canadian Journal of Psychology*, 19, 333–45.

NEISSER, U. (1967). *Cognitive Psychology*. New York, Appleton-Century-Crofts.

NELSON, T. O. and ROTHBART, R. (1972). Acoustic savings for items forgotten from long-term memory. *JEP*, 93, 357–60.

NORMAN, D. A. (1968). Toward a theory of memory and attention. *Psychological Review*, 75, 522–36.

OLSON, D. R. (1972). Language use for communicating, instructing, and thinking. In Carroll, J. B. and Freedle, R. O. (Eds). *Language Comprehension and the Acquisition of Knowledge*. Washington, D.C., Winston.

OSGOOD, C. E. (1970). Interpersonal verbs and interpersonal behaviour. In Cowan, J. L. (Ed.). *Studies in Thought and Language*. Tucson, University of Arizona Press.

OSGOOD, C. E., SUCI, G. J. and TANNENBAUM, P. H. (1957). *The Measurement of Meaning*. Urbana, University of Illinois Press.

PAIVIO, A. (1969). Mental imagery in associative learning and memory. *Psychological Review*, 76, 241–63.

PAIVIO, A. (1971a). Imagery and deep structure in the recall of English nominalisations. *JVLVB*, 10, 1–12.

PAIVIO, A. (1971b). *Imagery and Verbal Processes*. New York, Holt, Rinehart & Winston.

PAIVIO, A., YUILLE, J. C. and MADIGAN, S. A. (1968). Concreteness, imagery and meaningfulness values for 925 nouns. *JEP, Monograph Supplement*, 76, No.1, Part 2.

PERFETTI, C. A. (1969). Lexical density and phrase structure depth as variables in sentence retention. *JVLVB*, 8, 719–24.

PETERSON, L. R. and PETERSON, M. J. (1959). Short-term retention of individual verbal items. *JEP*, 58, 193–8.

POLLIO, H. R. (1968). Associative structure and verbal behavior. In Dixon, T. R. and Horton, D. L. (Eds). *Verbal Behavior and General Behavior Theory*. Englewood Cliffs, N. J., Prentice-Hall.

POLLIO, H. R., RICHARDS, S. and LUCAS, R. (1969). Temporal properties of category recall. *JVLVB*, 8, 529–36.

POSNER, M. I. (1969). Abstraction and the process of recognition. In Bower, G. H. and Spence, J. T. (Eds.). *The Psychology of Learning and Motivation*, Vol. III. New York, Academic Press.

POSNER, M. I. and WARREN, R. E. (1972). Traces, concepts, and conscious constructions. In Melton, A. W. and Martin, E. (Eds.). *Coding Processes in Human Memory*. Washington, D.C., Winston.

POSTMAN, L. (1968). Association and performance in the analysis of verbal learning In Dixon, T. R. and Horton, D. L. (Eds.). *Verbal Behavior and General Behavior Theory*. Englewood Cliffs, N.J., Prentice-Hall.

POSTMAN, L. (1969). Interference theory. In Talland, G. A. and Waugh, N. C. (Eds.). *The Pathology of Memory*. New York, Academic Press.

POSTMAN, L. (1971). Organization and interference. *Psychological Review*, 78, 290–302.

POSTMAN, L. (1972). A pragmatic view of organization theory. In Tulving, E. and Donaldson, W. A. (Eds.). *Organization of Memory*. New York, Academic Press.

POSTMAN, L. and PHILLIPS, L. W. (1965). Short-term temporal changes in free recall. *Quarterly Journal of Experimental Psychology*, 17, 132–8.

POSTMAN, L. and UNDERWOOD, B. J. (1973). Critical issues in interference theory. *Memory and Cognition*, 1, 19–40.

PRYTULAK, L. S. (1971). Natural language mediation. *Cognitive Psychology*, 2, 1–56.

PUFF, C. R. (1970a). Role of clustering in free recall. *JEP*, 86, 384–6.

PUFF, C. R. (1970b). An investigation of two forms of organization in free recall. *JVLVB*, 9, 720–4.

RAYMOND, B. (1969). Short-term and long-term storage in free recall. *JVLVB*, 8, 567–74.

REITMAN, W. (1970). What does it take to remember? In Norman, D. A. (Ed.). *Models of Human Memory*. New York, Academic Press.

RICHARDSON, J. (1972). Encoding and stimulus selection in paired-associate verbal learning. In Melton, A. W. and Martin, E. (Eds). *Coding Processes in Human Memory*. Washington, D.C., Winston.

ROHRMAN, N. L. (1968). The role of syntactic structure in the recall of English nominalisations. *JVLVB*, 7, 904–12.

ROHRMAN, N. L. (1970). More on the recall of nominalisations. *JVLVB*, 9, 534–6.

ROSENBERG, S. and JARVELLA, R. J. (1970). Semantic integration and sentence perception. *JVLVB*, 9, 548–53.

RUBENSTEIN, H., GARFIELD, L. and MILLIKAN, J. A. (1970). Homographic entries in the internal lexicon. *JVLVB*, 9, 487–92.

RUMELHART, D. E., LINDSAY, P. H. and NORMAN, D. A. (1972). A process model for long-term memory. In Tulving, E. and Donaldson, W. A. (Eds.). *Organization of Memory*. New York, Academic Press.

RUNDUS, D. (1971). Analysis of rehearsal processes in free recall. *JEP*, 89, 63–77.

RUNDUS, D. and ATKINSON, R. C. (1970). Rehearsal processes in free recall: a procedure for direct observation. *JVLVB*, 9, 99–105.

RUSSELL, W. A. and STORMS, L. H. (1955). Implicit verbal chaining in paired-associate learning. *JEP*, 49, 287–93.

SACHS, J. (1967). Recognition memory for syntactic and semantic aspects of connected discourse. *Perception and Psychophysics*, 2, 437–42.

SAVIN, H. B. and PERCHONOCK, E. (1965). Grammatical structure and the immediate recall of English sentences. *JVLVB*, 4, 348–53.

SCHAEFFER, B. and WALLACE, R. (1970). The comparison of word meanings. *JEP*, 86, 144–52.

SCHUBERT, R. E., LIVELY, B. L. and REUTENER, D. B. (1973). Release from proactive interference in the recall of sentences. *JEP*, 98, 423—5.

SHAFFER, W. O. and SHIFFRIN, R. M. (1972). Rehearsal and storage of visual information. *JEP*, 92, 292—6.

SHALLICE, T. and WARRINGTON, E. K. (1970). Independent functioning of verbal memory stores: a neuropsychological study. *Quarterly Journal of Experimental Psychology*, 22, 261—73.

SHUELL, T. J. (1969). Clustering and organisation in free recall. *Psychological Bulletin*, 72, 353—74.

SHULMAN, H. G. (1970). Encoding and retention of semantic and phonemic information in short-term memory. *JVLVB*, 9, 499—508.

SHULMAN, H. G. (1971). Similarity effects in short-term memory. *Psychological Bulletin*, 75, 399—414.

SHULMAN, H. G. (1972). Semantic confusion errors in short-term memory. *JVLVB*, 11, 221—7.

SILVERSTEIN, C. and GLANZER, M. (1971). Difficulty of a concurrent task in free recall: differential effects on STS and LTS. *Psychonomic Science*, 22, 367—8.

SLAMECKA, N. J. (1968). An examination of trace storage in free recall. *JEP*, 76, 504—13.

SLOBIN, D. I. (1971). *Psycholinguistics*. New York, Scott-Foresman.

SLOBIN, D. I. (1972). Seven questions about language development. In Dodwell, P. C.(Ed.). *New Horizons in Psychology*, Vol. 2. Harmondsworth, Penguin.

SNODGRASS, J. G. and JARVELLA, R. T. (1972). Some linguistic determinants of word classification times. *Psychonomic Science*, 27, 220—2.

SPERLING, G. (1960). The information available in brief visual presentations. *Psychological Monographs*, 74, 11 (Whole No. 498).

STANNERS, R. F. (1969). Grammatical organisation in free recall. *JVLVB*, 8, 95—100.

STERNBERG, S. (1966). High-speed scanning in human memory. *Science*, 153, 652—4.

STOFF, D. M. and EAGLE, M. N. (1971). The relationship among reported strategies, presentation rate, and verbal ability, and their effects on free recall learning. *JEP*, 87, 423—8.

STRAND, B. Z. (1970). Change of context and retroactive inhibition. *JVLVB*, 9, 202—6.

STRAND, B. Z. (1971). Further investigation of retroactive inhibition in categorized free recall. *JEP*, 87, 198—201.

TALLAND, G. (1968). Disorders of memory and learning. Harmondsworth, Penguin.

TELL, P. M. (1971). Influence of vocalization on short-term memory. *JVLVB*, 10, 149—56.

THOMPSON, C. P., HAMLIN, V. J. and ROENKER, D. L. (1972). A comment on the role of clustering in free recall. *JEP*, 94, 108—109.

THOMSON, D. M. and TULVING, E. (1970). Associative encoding and retrieval: weak and strong cues. *JEP*, 86, 255—62.

THURM, A. T. and GLANZER, M. (1971). Free recall in children: long-term store versus short-term store. *Psychonomic Science*, 23, 175—6.

TRABASSO, T. (1972). Mental operations in language comprehension. In Carroll, J. B. and Freedle, R. O.(Eds.). *Language Comprehension and the Acquisition of Knowledge*. Washington, D.C., Winston.

TREISMAN, A. M. (1969). Strategies and models of selective attention. *Psychological Review*, 76, 282—99.

TULVING, E. (1962). Subjective organisation in free recall of 'unrelated' words. *Psychological Review*, 69, 344—54.

TULVING, E. (1966). Subjective organisation and effects of repetition in multi-trial free-recall learning. *JVLVB*, 5, 193—8.

TULVING, E. (1968). Theoretical issues in free recall. In Dixon, T. R. and Horton, D. L. (Eds.). *Verbal Behavior and General Behavior Theory*. Englewood Cliffs, N.J., Prentice-Hall.

TULVING, E. (1972). Episodic and semantic memory. In Tulving, E. and Donaldson, W. A. (Eds.). *Organization of Memory*. New York, Academic Press.

TULVING, E. and MADIGAN, S. A. (1970). Memory and verbal learning. *Annual Review of Psychology*, 21, 437—84.

TULVING, E. and OSLER, S. (1968). Effectiveness of retrieval cues in memory for words. *JEP*, 77, 593—601.

TULVING, E. and PATTERSON, R. D. (1968). Functional units and retrieval processes in free recall. *JEP*, 77, 239—48.

TULVING, E. and PEARLSTONE, Z. (1966). Availability versus accessibility of information in memory for words. *JVLVB*, 5, 381—91.

TULVING, E. and PSOTKA, J. (1971). Retroactive inhibition in free recall: inaccessibility of information available in the memory store, *JEP*, 87, 1—8.

TULVING, E. and THOMSON, D. M. (1971). Retrieval processes in recognition memory: effects of associative context. *JEP*, 87, 116—24.

UNDERWOOD, B. J. (1948). Retroactive and proactive inhibition after 5 and 48 hours. *JEP*, 38, 29—38.

UNDERWOOD, B. J. (1963). Stimulus selection in verbal learning. In Cofer, C. N. and Musgrave, B. S. (Eds.). *Verbal Behavior and Learning: Problems and Processes*. New York, McGraw-Hill.

UNDERWOOD, B. J. (1965). False recognition by implicit verbal responses. *JEP*, 70, 122—9.

UNDERWOOD, B. J. (1969). Attributes of memory. *Psychological Review*, 76, 559—73.

UNDERWOOD, B. J. (1972). Are we overloading memory? In Melton, A. W. and Martin, E. (Eds.). *Coding Processes in Human Memory*. Washington, D.C., Winston.

UNDERWOOD, B. J. and EKSTRAND, B. R. (1968). Linguistic associations and retention. *JVLVB*, 7, 162—71.

UNDERWOOD, B. J., ZIMMERMAN, J. and FREUND, J. S. (1971). Retention of frequency information with observations on recognition and recall. *JEP*, 87, 149—62.

VOSS, J. F. (1972). On the relationship of associative and organisational processes. In Tulving, E. and Donaldson, W. A.(Eds.).*Organization of Memory*. New York, Academic Press.

WALLACE, W. P. (1970). Consistency of emission order in free recall. *JVLVB*, 9, 58–68.

WARR, P. B. (1973). Towards a more human psychology. *Bulletin of the British Psychological Society*, 26, 1–8.

WARRINGTON, E. K. (1971). Neurological disorders of memory. *British Medical Bulletin*, 27, 243–7.

WASON, P. C. (1965). The contexts of plausible denial. *JVLVB*, 4, 7–11.

WATKINS, M. J. (1972). Locus of the modality effect in free recall. *JVLVB*, 11, 644–8.

WAUGH, N. C. (1970). On the effective duration of a repeated word. *JVLVB*, 9, 587–95.

WAUGH, N. C. and NORMAN, D. A. (1965). Primary memory. *Psychological Review*, 72, 98–104.

WAUGH, N. C. and NORMAN, D. A. (1968). The measure of interference in primary memory. *JVLVB*, 7, 617–26.

WICKELGREN, W. A. (1965). Short-term memory for phonemically similar lists. *American Journal of Psychology*, 78, 567–74.

WICKELGREN, W. A. (1966). Distinctive features and errors in short-term memory for English consonants. *Journal of the Acoustical Society of America*, 39, 388–98.

WICKELGREN, W. A. (1967). Rehearsal grouping and the hierarchical organization of serial position cues in short-term memory. *Quarterly Journal of Experimental Psychology*, 19, 97–102.

WICKELGREN, W. A. (1969a). Context-sensitive coding, associative memory, and serial order in (speech) behavior. *Psychological Review*, 76, 1–15.

WICKELGREN, W. A. (1969b). Auditory and articulatory coding in verbal short-term memory. *Psychological Review*, 76, 232–5.

WICKENS, D. D. (1970). Encoding categories of words: An empirical approach to meaning. *Psychological Review*, 77, 1–15.

WICKENS, D. D. (1972). Characteristics of word encoding. In Melton, A. W. and Martin, E. (Eds.). *Coding Processes in Human Memory*. Washington, D.C., Winston.

WICKENS, D. D., BORN, D. G. and ALLEN, C. K. (1963). Proactive inhibition and item similarity in short-term memory. *JVLVB*, 2, 440–5.

WILKES, A. L. and KENNEDY, R. A. (1969). Relationship between pairing and retrieval latency in sentences of varying grammatical form. *JEP*, 79, 241–5.

WINOGRAD, E. (1968). List differentiation as a function of frequency and etention interval. *JEP Monographs*, 76, 2, 1–18.

WINOGRAD, E, (1972). *Understanding Natural Language*. New York, Academic Press. Also published in *Cognitive Psychology*, 3, 1–191.

WOLLEN, K. A. and LOWRY, D. H. (1971). Effects of imagery on paired-associate learning. *JVLVB*, 10, 276–84.

WOOD, G. (1969). Whole-part transfer from paired associate to free recall learning. *JEP*, **82**, 532–7.

WOOD, G. (1972). Organisational processes and free recall. In Tulving, E. and Donaldson, W. A. (Eds.).*\Organization of Memory*. New York, Academic Press.

YAVUZ, II. S. and BOUSFIELD, W. A. (1959). Recall of connotative meaning. *Psychological Reports*, **5**, 319–20.

YNGVE, V. (1960). A model and an hypothesis for language structure. *Proceedings of the American Philosophical Society*, **104**, 444–6.

YNTEMA, D. B. and TRASK, F. P. (1963). Recall as a search process. *JVLVB*, **2**, 65–74.

Subject Index

Author Index